In-and-Out

Amara Chidinma Ezediniru

In-and-Out
Copyright © Amara Chidinma Ezediniru 2018

ISBN 978-978-968-719-0

Cover design by Tope Akintayo

Printed and bound in Nigeria by D'Pedestal Communications Ltd.

Published by 

The moral of the author has been asserted.

1

In and Out

Appreciation

God, my ever-present help!

Ifeyinwa Gloria Ezediniru, your unwavering support astounds me. You proved that once a mum, always a mum. Thank you!

Chy, Obi, Kech, Uchay, Edo, Uju, Chybyk Ezediniru, Som and Nelo Agudosi – family is nothing without you.

Sam Otenaike – Thank you for your constant kind thoughts and for your fatherly counsel.

Victor Oluwasegun – You wholeheartedly went through the draft. You gave deep insights and guidance. Thank you for your amazing support.

Collins Chukwuemeka Nwaya – I was simply putting some thoughts to paper and you saw a book. You did not waver until the book came to be. Thank you!

Raymond J. Sefia – You stumbled on an error and immediately opted to edit this work. Your eagle eye and attention to detail is inspiring. Thank you, thank you, thank you!

Gibson Onyeka Egwudobi – Thank you for your love, support, humour and encouragement through the process of this book. You are deeply appreciated.

Rotary Club of Apo, Abuja – You are my family in diaspora. Thank you for making me stand tall.

In and Out

Prologue

Lying on my back in my big bed, I closed my eyes to see ahead. I usually did. The future refused to play out. I struggled again and again.

"Without the picture of where you are going, you may not recognize it when you get there", I reminisced on the preacher's voice of last Sunday. I did my best to see this future but I could not. Instead, tears flew through my eyes unstoppably. Those eyes were still closed. I lay still in my bed and was oblivious to my surroundings.

I was used to seeing myself and how I would rather spend the rest of my days on earth. I had imagined all kinds of things and events. I had seen myself with diverse people - good, successful, rich, beautiful, intelligent, classy, to mention a few. In my new world, I was allergic to negativity. The only time I came close to unwholesomeness was to help the downtrodden get justice and the poor attain their dreams. I was an unapologetic philanthropist; doing good was my real nature. I spoke for the maltreated widows and single mums. My voice came down hard on injustice of any sort. I was an advocate of a fair Nigeria. I did this effortlessly.

That day was different, all my pictures were lost. They were replaced with tears, while haziness was rather vivid. As my mind warred, my body was still, you would have thought I was dead. According to Kamsi who was observing me for a while, "I could not unravel what was going on, I thought you were gone." In fear, he held

In and Out

on watching. He took a picture of me as proof. He was going to have me tell him what happened when I finally came out of my tranquil state.

As he recounted his part of the story, I was grateful he had not interrupted me. I was thankful for his patience and his thoughtfulness. Kamsi is rather a deep teenager. He understood what being alone meant, he enjoyed having such quiet moments to himself. His confusion was not only in knowing that his mum also had hers but that it could get intense and lost. "I touched your legs and you did not move, I bent towards your face and saw your tears and I knew you were alive. I imagined you had soul-traveled so I pulled a chair and decided to wait on you through the journey. I had to quickly take a picture to avoid denial", he said.

It was a very long trip.

I did not just see pictures, I saw a movie, an unedited movie of myself and how it all began …

"Welcome back", he said.

I turned my head to see him sitting by me raptly focused. "Welcome back? How do you mean?" I asked with a surprised face.

"You were gone for quite a while, how was your journey?" he asked.

"What journey? I simply took a nap."

"Not so, mum. I have been sitting here for over an hour. Look, I took many pictures of you. I was afraid but for the fact that your eyes were twitching and the tears wouldn't stop. I knew you were either dreaming or in a trance of sorts. Whichever it was, there was a lot of

In and Out

emotion involved. Welcome back", he concluded. "I wish you could trust me and share. I am a man, the only man in your life."

I was stunned. I looked at him with admiration. Did I raise this son single handedly? I asked myself. This is a good job I have done. I praised myself. "You will read it, it is a book. Patience please", I assured him.

In and Out

1

MY ABODE

"King sized bed, white sheets, soft pillow, at least four."

"The texture?"

"Soft, cotton, silk, satin, erm, make a choice for me, please."

"The room, any preferences?"

"Like perfume, drapes, light, flooring, which am I permitted to change?"

"All madam, all. We can even change the wall paper, chandelier, whatever you want."

"So be it then. Make the room blue, sky blue. I want to feel like I'm in heaven's love garden."

"Alright ma'am. I'll get our creative team to work. When is the date please?"

"My birthday."

"What date, ma'am?"

"You mean you don't know my birth date?"

"I got it, my apologies. How long please?"

"One week. That should be enough, right?"

"Certainly ma'am."

"Alright then. I 'll wait for your call."

"Sure. Thank you, ma'am."

"Um, one minute please."

"Yes, ma'am."

"What range of exotic cars do you have?"

"Audi, BMW, Bugatti Chiron, Bentley, Dodge, Ferrari, Koenigsegg, Lamborghini. Would you like me to send a catalogue, ma'am?"

"That will be greatly appreciated, thanks."

"Alright then. Is there anything else?"

"Yes, please. Who are the drivers?"

"Their profiles with their schedules will be sent too, you can make your choice."

"Thank you for your time."

"The pleasure is mine, ma'am."

I smiled sheepishly. I loved it there. I was in total control. Everyone waited on me. My wish was their command.

"What else?" I soliloquized. "I hope I'm not missing out on anything. I want this to be the fairest of them all." I stood by the window. I could see the blue sky and the beach and happy couples. I'd

In and Out

rather live the rest of my life happy and safe in this exotic resort with all the attendants at my beck and call. It's simply heavenly!

It was the early hours of the morning. It was a bit too early for breakfast. I was already up as my manner was. Those days, I got up first to make my regular soul travels. My journey could last for up to an hour. Most often, I returned uninterrupted filled with gladness.

"Good morning, sis."

"Good morning, Di. How are you today?"

"Very well, thank you", I responded as I got ready for work.

I had moved in with my sister soon after my marriage breakdown. Having no money to rent a new apartment, I figured that living with my sister and putting some savings together, I could sort my accommodation problem as fast as possible. I was that determined. I worked hard and saved even harder! I rose to catch the earliest bus, walked some distance, took another bus and then walked some more. This routine kept me fit and slim, it saved a lot on transport too.

As I walked through the streets to work, I could not help but admire the luxury homes I passed by. I worked in a school located in one of the city's choice areas. Minister's Hill in Maitama District was not for everybody. The bourgeois lived there. I promised myself to get to the top by my own sweat this time. Depending on a man to bridge the wealth gap was a complete waste of time. I recalled how lots of women who'd married to escape poverty had ended up miserable in the riches. Some girls were raised in this clime as property or trophies for men to eventually acquire. Another set was raised to be negotiation tools out of poverty. Either way, the men knew this. We also knew it. Only a few parents with illumination understood that the girl child is as

In and Out

valuable as the male counterpart. Going to work every morning gave me hope. Looking at the houses and the exotic cars kept me alive and optimistic. It assuaged my daily long treks. Sometimes, I was saddened by the fact that I was living an impoverished life. This sadness fueled my resolve to become financially empowered as soon as possible. I had been used to driving or being driven for over ten years, and now, here I was starting my life all over again, this time, worse than I ever was. I sang when in a good mood and prayed as I navigated the narrow pathway in the mornings. My prayers were no longer the way I had learnt. It was more conversational and sounded like wishes. Sometimes, I voiced out loudly, other times, I was silent. I imagined myself living in one of those houses and commanding great wealth. My mind was my gateway to anywhere. I was everything I wanted to be, thanks to my imagination. The pictures were vivid. I got to work before a quarter past six in the morning. I was an hour early. I was a workhorse.

Nyere, my sister, did her best taking care of me. Besides providing food and clothes, she was trustworthy company. Nyere would never disclose my situation to anyone. Nyere supported me all round - morally, financially and spiritually. She looked at my countenance and took care never to offend me implicitly or otherwise. We lived happily together. Nyere was a super sister.

One Sunday morning, I buried my head under my pillow. This was sometimes my position when I embarked on my imaginary journeys. To me, this was freedom. I did not require money, connections, visa and all the hullabaloo associated with travels across borders. I simply took a comfortable position and zoomed off in a minute. I saw myself as a private jet owner being taken to all parts of the world. I used electric carts across the mountains of Kilimanjaro. I lived in a ship and cruised through the Atlantic. I was on all the

In and Out

continents and in as many countries as I had heard of. Sometimes, I wished not to return.

That morning, as I buried my head under the pillow, there were sounds. As usual, I was alone with Nyere. It was a small studio apartment, and so the kitchen and toilet were not that big. My sister told of how she paused and listened more, unsure of what sound it was and where it was coming from. To her, I was asleep. She listened again and was without any doubt that she heard a sobbing sound.

"Oh dear, Di, not again. When will this crying stop? You can't keep living this way, it doesn't change anything. Please stop, and let's find a way to keep you occupied", she consoled. The sob's pitch was increasing slightly as the consolation continued. In a matter of seconds, I was crying inconsolably. This gave Nyere a clue of what happened whenever I took this position. She kept an eye on me the more, especially whenever I was quiet.

The posture of a pillow over the head on a bed was no longer to be. Nyere would pull the pillow off and demand for a change. She never wanted to see her younger sister cry, not for anything or anyone. "Di, you must move on with life. You can't possibly mourn forever." Nyere was getting tired of repeating the same encouraging words.

Sometimes, I thought Nyere did not understand how I felt. I did not only lose a marriage, but I also lost a home. My children were separated from their father whom they loved very much. My heart tore each time I looked at them and saw their confusion. It was not simply the end of an abusive relationship, I mourned the loss of ten precious years. I could have achieved more with those years had we been compatible. I know myself. I am good hearted. I am full of potential. I thought Eka was too. I had not considered the loss of my personal

10

effects yet. I did not leave with the least of my belongings; not even the pieces of jewellery I loved the most nor my beautiful dresses, some of which I was yet to complete payment for. There were pictures of me before marriage, gifts, letters, clothing accessories, a whole lot of tiny things that brought smiles to my face. I was yet to consider household items that I bought from my little savings. They were of incalculable worth. I did not have a lot in my collection hence each item was valuable. Each had a special story. Losing them was losing my life. I grieved as though I lost a life. I probably did.

Nyere was a bit older than me. She had never married. She'd had her fair share of betrayals from the men she loved and dated. Some of them did not consider her good enough for marriage. Our mother discouraged her about a few, due to ethnic and religious differences, while some were nothing close to her kind of man. She did not believe every woman had to be married. I considered her weird because of this. Nyere wished to have a child but not necessarily a husband. This was a tough pill for our family to swallow. Our dissent did not dissuade her from looking out for a worthy man. She was unwilling to compromise her standards regarding a male companion. She had her screening skills. She knew how to eliminate the unserious ones. My presence in her house temporarily halted all kinds of visitors. She wanted a comfort zone for me and sufficient time to heal. We both believed that staying away from people at that time was therapeutic.

My abode, my place of comfort was demolished by Nyere, my sister.

11

2

MY FLASH IN THE PAN LOVE

Eka was the love of my life, and I was his. We told each other very many nice stories and shared our thoughts. We talked about our dreams and aspirations. We had names for the three children we were going to have. We even used the first two letters of their names to form the name of a company we registered. We prayed together sometimes, we ate together other times.

That night after our traditional marriage, we made love like never before. I consider it the most memorable night with Eka. In the morning, we made a pact enthused by our love. We promised never to hurt nor leave each other. We were going to always be there for each other. We would be honest in our dealings and be transparent too. Eka had told a few lies while we dated. That night, I reminded him that there would be no more lies between us. He concurred as we concluded the pact with the blood from the tips of our thumbs. We curled in each other's arms and felt very safe. I recall as tears flowed from my eyes, making those lovely promises staring directly into his eyes. He was man enough not to cry. He was calm and consoling. For me, I just began a journey of no return. I started another phase of life. Eka was going to be my world. I would consider him before anything and anyone else. I would make him my priority. I would be submissive and loving. I would serve him diligently. I would be the definition of a

12

wife to him. It was a misty December morning, few days after Christmas. The mood was still ebullient. We were locked up in our little room of love, making endless promises to each other.

About ten o'clock that morning, I came outside. The compound was earthen while the houses were made of concrete blocks. A typical village house of an upcoming man. It was Eka's family house. His father built it in his heyday. As soon as I stepped out, I headed for where the broom was in a different corner of the premises. There were pockets of structures accommodating different relations and things, some with a thatched roof, others with zinc.

Ndem was Eka's grandmother, a humorous pragmatic woman. Grandma Ndem was sitting outside already. She had a permanent position from where she could see every movement. She was a matriarch indeed, absolutely in charge of the home and everyone. Her word was law. Everyone respected her not only for being the eldest but for her realistic views. Once I stepped out of our flat, my face met hers.

"Good morning, mama."

"Good morning Dinma, *ibolachi*?"

"Yes, *nnem*."

As we exchanged pleasantries, I was heading for the broom place which also looked like I was coming to her. Her position was indeed central.

"*Ebe ka I na-ga?*"

"I need a broom, I would like to sweep the compound."

"Which compound? go back to the room!"

13

In and Out

"Mama *isi gini*?" I was utterly startled by her remark. I was not sure if I had offended or not.

"I said go back to the room and stay with your husband. They will clean the compound, don't worry."

I stood still for a while; she pushed.

"*Asi m gi ba n'ulo*. Go, go back in." This time, she motioned with her hands and her voice a bit louder. I understood her insistence. I smiled.

"*Dalu, dalu*", I said as I went back to be with Eka.

I narrated the short episode to him. He was very pleased. He gave a shrill laughter. "I told you, she likes you. My family likes you", Eka said. I was the happiest bride at that moment. What else would a wife ask for besides a man that loved her genuinely and a family that gave her an unconditional acceptance? I was over the moon. "I must remain 'homely', I thought to myself as I jumped back into his arms.

In our part of the world, a good woman ought to be 'homely'. Being 'homely' means doing all the house chores impeccably well and without prompting. She must be submissive and enduring. Her loyalty should be to her husband's family. She is to literally worship them. She is to be seen and not heard. She should be a great cook; clean spotlessly and has a good attitude. Our 'homely' woman is the woman who knows to look away conveniently. She is not allowed to dream big. She must regard her husband as a lord and master. She forgives easily and is indefatigable. A 'homely' woman does not need to have a great fashion sense. She must be modest in taste. To us, a woman is 'homely' when she is subservient. She is not to have a say in anything except when invited. The 'homely' woman has no need of education. Her certificate is useless if she cannot cook and clean. She has no

In and Out

business with neither science nor law. At most, she can get involved in petty trading. She is expected to maintain absolute silence; this silence is regarded as respect. This 'homely' woman must be fertile. Her virtues will mean nothing if she is unable to have children.

When a man wants to marry, he will have to let his bride-to-be meet his family. At this meeting, the lady is tested in various forms. One of the tests includes waking up early, sweeping the house and making a tasty breakfast for the household. She is keenly watched. Most women strive to be 'homely' since they are raised to view marriage as the apex of life's achievement. We spent about a week in the family house; the yuletide was over and the New Year day had passed too. Everyone treated me with love and respect. We were leaving back to the city with fervor. On a personal note, I was more resolved to be submissive to this new family.

Love is life and life is good.

Eka was everything good that January. We discussed his big dreams for us. We reiterated the number of children we would have including their gender. In our imagination, we were a couple to emulate. I wrote him love letters every day. I sent some as short messages to his phone and the rest were paper based. When I got home before him, I dropped them where he would see them. Sometimes, I made our bed and spread red petals on it before he got back from work. Other times, we came home together like inseparable love birds. Everyone in our circle knew we were the bubbly and exemplary couple! In our minds, at least in mine, that was the goal and I was giving it my very best shot.

I recall his first trip to Dubai few weeks after we became a couple. I had the pleasure of packing his suitcase, deciding his

In and Out

wardrobe for the duration of his stay. This was my first experience living with a man that I called mine. I was bent on being optimistic the long haul. Every little thing had so much meaning to me. It mattered that I selected his clothes and washed his underwear. I was enthralled to serve him breakfast in bed and remove his shoes once he got back from work. I was his launderer - washing, starching, ironing, arranging his wardrobe were my duties. I discharged them with utmost delight. He was my man, my king, my lord and I enjoyed serving him. It was indeed my pleasure! Eka basked in these.

Our sex was voluptuary. He knew what to touch and when to touch. The kisses were passionate and the feelings during foreplay were indescribable. It didn't take much to thrill me in bed. Eka got me well in this.

At the shop, I was his staff. I treated him as a boss. When he called, I would respond with 'yes sir'. There were never arguments. I worked like any other staff. I maintained the books and retained the customers. I proposed ideas and followed them through. Eka was my world; I was determined to give him the best of times as long as I was his wife. When we had misunderstandings, I was quick to apologise. I felt it was my duty to so do. I met his business partners. We worked seamlessly. The business grew. Our love grew. So, I thought.

Eka called me a special name. I was always dazzled hearing that name from his voice. The texture, the tone, the modulation, the name, everything about him calling that name was musical and magical. I was always swept off my feet. My face literally glowed. Even a child could see the deep blush that spread on my dark cheeks the moment I heard the name. I had not decided what special name to call him. He meant different things at different times. One name could not capture it at all. I called him all manner of loveliness, from Sweet

In and Out

to Allure, to King, to Love, to Mine, to *Obim*, the names were just insufficient. All the obstacles I'd experienced during our cohabiting days seemed to have vanished. There was peace, perhaps because I had finally become his. His seal of ownership was boldly printed on my forehead the day he handed my bride price to my kinsmen. Eka was sweet, loving and everything in between those first few months of legitimately being under the same roof.

Having returned to the city, his family gave us sufficient space to lead our new lives together. His mum called occasionally to ensure all was well. Ndem was quite old. She rarely called but her greetings were promptly and lovingly dispatched to me. Both women subtly asked how my body was 'doing me'. This was a nice way of finding out if an offspring was on the way.

By the third month, I took ill with malaria. It was a horrible attack. I had never experienced malaria in that form. It shook my very foundation and brought me completely down. I recall how Eka rushed me to the hospital and I was placed on admission. "She must have taken in", Nne told Eka. Even the neighbours who already had children opined so. Everyone encouraged him and started to congratulate him in advance. They extolled him … 'you are a great man, a sharp shooter'. His head was swollen. He was so confident of himself and his ability.

"Everyone thinks you are pregnant."

"Pregnant? How can this be pregnancy?"

"Ike said this was how it happened to his wife the first time."

"Really? 'I finished my menstruation a few days ago. It can't possibly be pregnancy."

"You never know. God's miracle defies science sometimes."

17

In and Out

"Not in this case. Please, what did the doctor say?"

"He said the result is not out."

"What test did he run?"

"I haven't checked, I will go to see him from here but please pull yourself together. I am sure you are pregnant, everyone cannot be wrong. Even Mama Onyinye said so and grandma Ndem, too. All these women have experience and they cannot be wrong."

I spent two nights at the hospital. It was a private hospital so I had my room. I enjoyed the services. I praised Eka for bringing me to such a place. It must have cost him a lot. I was discharged on the third day without being pregnant. I was surprised at the insinuation of being pregnant but more astonished when I overheard Eka reporting his observation of the doctor to one of our neighbours, Ike.

"That doctor is stupid."

"Why do you say so?"

"Do you know that he didn't even conduct a pregnancy test until I asked him to?"

"You don't say!"

"He apologized to me that this could have been pregnancy but the antibiotics he administered were heavy and could have made her lose the baby."

"I don't understand you, say it again."

"As soon as we arrived at the hospital, he started giving her antibiotics. He started treating malaria. He even said he suspected tuberculosis because she was coughing incessantly. It was at my instance that he

In and Out

did a pregnancy test after the second day. He said it could have been pregnancy and he was sorry he didn't have a pregnancy test done first."

"Noooooo, that man is reputable. His hospital is reputable. He cannot possibly be that negligent."

"I will never go there again. He is incompetent, he is a stupid man. His hospital is not even cheap. How can I spend so much to treat common malaria?"

I felt really sorry for the poor doctor and became more worried about the man I married. Eka went on and on about the doctor's ineptitude, carelessness and inexperience. I could not juxtapose this level of shallow mindedness. How could he be making such inferences? What was his basis? I was called back to reality. This married Eka is no different from the one I cohabited with. He broke the news of my hospital discharge to his nuclear and extended family. Everyone was calling to console. They all had the undertone of 'another baby will come' as they spoke individually. I was perplexed! I knew I was in for big trouble if I did not get pregnant as soon as possible. Eka and I had spent a whole year living together before taking the giant step. Not one day did my period delay. I became worried. The honey moon period was over and everyone was expecting result of the work done.

In and Out

3

CONFUSED IDENTITY, THE MARSIN STORY

It was a hot afternoon, the peak of summer, the heat was scorching and the streets were lonely. I'd just come out from the bank hoping to catch a taxi.

"Where to?" asked the driver of a car that screeched to a halt in front of me.

"Federal Housing."

"Get in."

"Thanks."

I knew this was not a taxi, the car, the driver, the presentation all implied so. Except for very few, most cab men I had seen did not consider it necessary to take care of either themselves or their cars. This was before Uber imposed its presence on commuters within the city.

"I couldn't bear seeing such a beautiful lady stand in this sun."

"Very thoughtful of you, sir. Thank you."

"I'm Sam."

"Di."

"It's a pleasure."

There was silence.

20

In and Out

The drive was smooth, the music was low. The car interior was clean and looked well maintained. The air conditioning was soothing. The driver sized up his new companion. He was a bit unsure of where to begin from. Indeed, I am a beautiful woman with an imposing frame. My chocolate skin, slim and tall physique could have stood me out more like a beauty queen or royalty. I am charismatic; my smile is broad and pleasant. I am highly extroverted and can easily adjust to any situation. I am a realist, never putting on a façade.

"Erm, are you married?"

"What?" I was utterly stunned. I didn't expect this sort of question on a very hot afternoon. To think that many of my compliments included not looking like a mother. I was taken aback by his question. It was less than six months after a noxious marriage breakup whose reality I was beginning to accept.

"No … eeeerrrrm, I mean yes, actually no", I floundered.

Sam's eyes pierced at me by the corner. His countenance gave away his confusion. He was unsure what I was hiding; married women take pride in showing off their status. He must have smelt a rat.

For the very first time, life was neither black nor white. It was not hot or cold. It was confusion. I could not help it. This had been my dilemma.

"I didn't get you." Sam sought clarity.

"I am MARSIN."

"Say it again."

21

In and Out

"Please take your right, then your left, we are almost there."

"I will not be able to drive into the Estate; can I drop you by the gate?" The Estate as we fondly called it was a very large walled community with over two hundred spacious houses.

"That's alright. Let's use the first gate then."

Soon we were by the Estate's first gate. It was usually locked by that time of the day to check for charlatans. Residents knew that cars were not allowed to drive in during working hours using the first gate; pedestrians could walk in. It was not out of place to have cars drop their passengers by the gate. Some cars actually parked waiting for pick-ups.

Sam took the cue, he approached the first gate slowly. He seemed intrigued already. He probably was not sure what sense to make of the word 'marsin'. I believe he was unclear what he heard and did not know the best way to ask without offending his passenger.

"It would be nice to see you again."

"Sure, of course."

"Care if I get your number?"

"0805 ......9."

"When can I call you?"

"Whenever."

"I hope your husband will not mind."

"There is no husband!" I retorted vehemently.

"Alright then, bye", Sam gently withdrew.

22

Sam must have recognized something was definitely wrong. As he drove away, I knew he was not going to make further contact except he was an angel. Despite being a beautiful lady, I was a bit unkempt. He possibly could guess what the problem was but did not look like he could be my saviour. I believed Sam was a married man looking for a hit and run available lass.

I got home in a state; threw myself on the bed and started sobbing immediately. "A man poses a simple question and my world crumbles", I thought deeply. I became melancholic and as usual went hard on myself.

"It's your fault. You could have stayed. You could have borne it. It wasn't that bad, at least he didn't kill you. There were just little lies here and there", I blasted myself. "How about the cheating and the beating?" an inner voice whispered. "All men cheat, that should not make you quit. You are strong. You are prayerful. You should have continued praying. What is your testimony now? You are neither married nor single. As for the beating, you should have stayed out of his way. You brought this upon yourself, deal with it." my fight continued. I was getting loud, neighbours would have noticed a bit of the drama. Unfortunately, Nyere was still at work. There was no one to stop this venom I was spitting on myself. I continued to slap and mock me. I got up and stood in front of the mirror. The only word to define my state was deranged. I was merciless. I cursed the person in the mirror with all my might and then completely broke down in tears.

I did not plan for an abrupt end. Everything looked alright. We were envied. He loved me, so he said. And I was happy to believe. There were occasional storms. We sailed through one after another. The tears were uncontrollable as I reminisced on my marriage; his words, his gifts, his smiles, his hugs, his kisses, the play, his deeds and

23

In and Out

the pleasures. But the pictures of his lies, his betrayals, his punches, his lock-ups were too intense. I cried until I drifted into a deep slumber.

"What status is marsin and for how long will you live in this illusion?" Nyere asked as we recounted the events of the day.

"Married single, until the court acts."

"The courts are very sluggish, damn too slow."

"Not the court yet, we haven't even gone to court. I learnt that we have to be apart for not less than a year before we start the divorce process. It's just about 6 months now."

"So, you will keep being marsin till then?"

"That's my cross, what can I do? And I must not be seen in any suggestive manner with a man, too. This is another prison."

"Oh dear!"

We both eventually got busy with other activities. I was learning to settle down to the life of a single woman after more than ten years of total commitment and dedication to my lord and husband. Poor me, I did not envisage this in my life's path, not with all my dedication and faithful service to God. I prayed fervently. I believed God would perform a miracle of a change of heart for Eka, my estranged husband. This secret thought was not to be known to anyone who knew me. Though I was out of the abusive relationship, it was still in me. My mind was yet to be freed. I barely kept a bright face.

One thing however gladdened my heart. I was still beautiful enough to attract a man, not just any man. A man with Sam's specification was well above average. He spoke with finesse. He was cultured. He was well dressed. His car exuded freshness. This was priceless for me. I went down memory lane on how I had spent my life in the past ten or more years. I knew I goofed woefully. I had no confidant apart from my sister, Nyere. Nyere was not allowed to disclose my situation. I did not even tell her everything that a confidant should have been told. Our mother did not know how my marriage fared. I had only church sisters in my life who abandoned me at my lowest moment. I was down. I would be up, I was convinced about this.

In and Out

4

WORK, WORK, WORK

With two children and myself and no support from Eka, I knew I had to work extremely hard. My family provided the needed emotional succour, but unfortunately, no member was buoyant enough to help with my financial responsibilities. It was the fear of survival that kept me in the abusive relationship for as long as it lasted.

Less than one year into the marriage, I was pregnant with a set of twins. I was not working and he didn't even want me to work. The quest to keep busy made me join in his business. Eka had an electronic shop he ran with a sales girl. The business was wrapped around him and merely thrived like a one-man business should. I was not proud of working in a shop. I had bigger dreams. My first major problem in the marriage had just set in. I was not to work for anyone. If I must work, then it had to be for my lord. I suggested being paid a monthly salary considering that I was bringing in my expertise in Customer Relations and general Business Management and these were beginning to positively affect the business. He reluctantly agreed to pay. He did this for two months only.

I understood lack in the midst of plenty. Eka's business steadily improved. He would however, not allow his wife enjoy the benefits of being a businessman's dependent, employee and fellow labourer. We toiled together to make the shop grow and it indeed grew. We moved from one shop to two and from being in a small shop at the back of the building to a very strategic bigger front shop. Our setting changed from the shop of a petty trader in the commercial city of Nnewi to a finely planned retail store. I brought in the grandeur. I aimed at attracting the elites and dared to be different from his counterparts in his line of business. They were mainly traders. Eka was educated and so was I. I figured we could make a difference. If I could not work in my dream office, I could turn what we had to my dream then. I simply did not realise how much work carrying him along was. Considering that I did not make the final decisions and did not control the finances, this was onerous! The picture I was painting took time to be understood by him.

He was very careful about whatever amount he sent me to the market with. I gave a full satisfactory account else I risked not getting more. Eka was a perfect remote control. He planned every activity involving cash. He belonged to an obscure reasoning of not letting a woman own money. To him, when a woman owned a lot of money, she became uncontrollable and insubordinate. I tried to wriggle out of this mindset. It was always one of our major dissensions. When I went to the hairdresser's, he paid her directly. If there was to be a trip abroad, he made all the arrangement down to the hotel and paid directly. He paid the children's fees directly. He bought most of their things. All the alternative avenues a typical Nigerian wife makes money from her husband were fully under his control. Sometimes, I wondered if he had the tertiary education he said he did. If I needed clothes, I could scout for a seller that will either deliver to the house so that Eka paid him directly or waited until he saw what he liked in his own time. My wardrobe was managed by him. Eka took pride in buying my clothes. Unfortunately, he bought to his bland fashion taste or perhaps, he was intentionally ensuring his wife did not appear trendy.

"Don't you know you are a married woman? There is a way to dress", he usually said. I was not allowed to wear knee-length dresses, fitted pair of jeans, sleeveless tops, knee length skirts, shorts and

In and Out

anything that flaunted my beauty. I could wear flowing gowns, long skirts, wrappers and the likes. No part of my skin was allowed to show yet we were not Muslims. The unwritten rule was that 'to wear something trendy, then I must either be with the children or with him'. I was not allowed to dress up well and leave the house alone. "I don't want men chasing after you, you are my *Agbani Darego*", he would say.

Initially, I did my best to conform. First, I thought it was love. Then I considered it not a high price to pay for a successful marriage. Indeed, I could have given up more. I conformed without a fight. I was a good Christian girl; dressing properly was my identity naturally. However, I realised much later that there was much more to this, it was an unhealthy show of power. It was neither borne out of love nor genuine interest to protect me. I think Eka simply wanted to show his sovereignty. He even demanded that I called him lord, citing the biblical Sarah as an example.

It was tragic to have this man have absolute control over the family purse. I realised this after marriage. At first, it was amusing and unbelievable then it became frustrating and devastating. I became completely broken. What else could I do? I needed to work, to make my own living. I needed to have my money, worked for by me, paid into my account and spent by me. As a younger single lady, this was easier. Right after my National Youth Service Programme, I did not relent in getting a job immediately. I applied everywhere, I checked the dailies. I kept my ears to the ground. I attended several interviews until I finally got a job in Abuja. I had just myself and my box of a few clothes. It was easy to hitchhike and cohabit with friends. I had no responsibilities, no one to clothe, feed, shelter and worry about. I dated as suited and spent my time as I deemed fit. With two children to

In and Out

*Agbani Darego is the first native African to win Miss World contest.

constantly worry about, life as a single mum was certainly not a walk in the park. My predicament was just unfolding.

Fear gripped me. The fear of failing. The fear of lacking. The fear of begging. Most of all was the fear of not having the custody of my children. Some people had informed me that not having a means of income could tilt the court's decision against me when we head for a formal dissolution. I was determined to do everything I could, to make ends meet.

I had two family members in Abuja, Nyere and Culeta. I was living with Nyere, she had been tremendously supportive. Her acts were beyond my imagination. She taught me the meaning of empathy, tolerance, kindness and everything on that spectrum in actions. She simply did not have the financial wit. I could not burden her any further. Culeta showed some degree of willingness to help me with some money just at the beginning of the end with Eka.

I was directed to Barrister Martins by my friend Efe. Barrister Martins had helped Efe's close friend get a satisfactory divorce and win a custody battle for her daughter. I was too naïve, I did not understand the rigors a divorce process portended. I also was in limbo about the cost. As soon as it dawned on me that the marriage had hit the rocks, I started talking to a few friends, church friends. As expected, the very few were petrified. "My friend is going through a lot, I am making inquiries for her", I would say. Efe was the only church friend that gave me a full nod. Efe was a so-to-say non-conformist church member.

Efe had her marital issues. She separated from her man for a year or so before relocating to London. Her marriage was salvaged however. She understood my predicament more than I did. Efe was a

In and Out

fashion guru with her fashion label. Often times, I would tell her, "Eka did not allow me to wear that beautiful dress you made". She knew perfectly what I was going through. Helping me source for a lawyer was delightful.

Barrister Martins' bill was four hundred and fifty thousand naira. He asked for an initial deposit of fifty thousand to begin the paper work and the rest to be spread as the matter progressed. I did not have such an amount, not even anything close to it. I called Culeta.

Culeta was older than Nyere. She was doing very well as a banker. She promised to send at least thirty thousand naira immediately. I was elated. I waited. After two days, I called my sister to ascertain the situation. "I am sorry, Di; my husband and I do not believe in divorce. We are Christians. We are of the Household of Faith denomination. We are even deacons. My husband said I should not give you any money. Giving you money means that I am encouraging you and we cannot encourage you", Culeta continued her sermon from the other end of the telephone. "Alright, thank you", I responded without letting her preaching continue and the call ended. That was the end of our relationship. Culeta did not bother about how I fared thereafter. She was the only sibling who clearly could help but declined.

From some sort of luxury to the streets, from driving a posh car to using bikes and trekking, from wearing new clothes to using *okirika* - a term used for second hand clothes, from a spacious three bedroom flat in a choice city area to a studio apartment in the ghetto. The transition was swift and absurd. The thoughts of it made me cry daily. I was an integral part of growing the wealth. I did not meet Eka a rich man. We toiled together. To me, I was building a dynasty with my husband. To him, he may have seen a hardworking woman he could

In and Out

use. The pictures of my hard work even with the pregnancy were as clear in my head. The business was a baby as well. We were trying to grow it in the right direction. He had a 'parlour business' (small business owner mentality) in mind while I dreamt far bigger. As the big dreamer, I had to keep juggling the home and the workplace. I did not just provide management; I brought in customers from my former place of work, one of whom was Dr. Shehu.

Dr. Shehu worked in a government department. We were waiting for an opportunity to do some government contracts. Hopes were high on both sides until I lost the job. I married Eka and we began building our business together. One day, Dr. Shehu walked into our electronics shop. He was surprised to see me and I inevitably introduced him to my husband. This was the beginning of our business breakthrough. Dr. Shehu signed off some contracts for us continuously. I stepped aside from the relationship, naturally. It was men's affair. A typical northerner would rather deal with a man except the girl was his lover.

I have always worked hard. I never looked back once I got on the plough. Work became my life. I worked and saved and hoped.

By the fourth month, I got a better house in a gated community, not like a ghetto. My self-esteem began to rise. The accommodation itself was not super but the environment was. I could proudly tell anyone I lived in 'Federal Housing'. It would not matter that there was no mattress, no pillows, no television, no floor covering, no couch and the basic home furniture. My bed was made of cartons. I moved Nyere with me. None of us should live in the ghetto. Life was looking brighter.

31

Soon, I bought a taxi with the loan my boss granted me. My income was growing. I took up extra work. I worked from 6:00am to 7:00pm, sometimes 8pm, Monday to Saturday and some few hours on Sunday. My struggle to live above waters was real. Besides me, there were two children to feed, clothe, shelter and school. I considered myself too intelligent to fail.

As each day progressed, I got better at the job. This was in practice, my first real job as a teacher. The first time I got a job as an administrative staff in a primary school was the beginning of the end of my marriage. I learnt this from my neighbour, Oge. By the time it dawned on me that Eka was no longer interested in the marriage, I began to speak out. I started asking for help. Many of my friends were shocked because we seemed perfect. There was no inclination of war and to think an end was suddenly here, they could not fathom. It was in this quest for help that Oge informed me what Eka told her husband.

"He said that the moment you insisted that you will work in that school and you started work, the marriage ended", said Oge.

"But this was four years ago", I replied.

"Well, that's what he told my husband, I don't know but I think that man is wicked and callous. He keeps dragging my husband along for his escapades. My husband keeps declining, telling him that he doesn't lead such life. My husband doesn't even like him."

"Thank you so much. At least I have an idea of what is going on, thank you."

The only reason he did not want a working wife was to enjoy absolute power and control of our home. No sane mind understood this thought process.

In and Out

Now, as an inexperienced teacher, I had the limited option to train myself. I read vast and wide. I surfed the internet and watched lots of videos on YouTube. Luckily, Nyere had been teaching for a while. There was a coach right in our room! I made use of every opportunity to become better in my new career. In less than six months, I was promoted from an assistant teacher to a class teacher, and my salary was raised by forty five percent. This was the first time that school was doing such. They simply had to reward my dynamism and dedication. I was an exemplary teacher. I did not just do my basic roles well; I opened two more revenue opportunities for the school. I introduced a Saturday Learning Support Programme for children with learning difficulties. Parents paid separately for this. I also introduced discovery and adventure club for children whose parents left in school till 6:00pm daily.

As more revenue came in, I determined to engage in international professional development. I already had a visa to England. Thankfully, this was one of the perks from my estranged marriage. I worked and saved and travelled for a week-long training. It was highly celebrated. This effort stood me out amongst my colleagues and endeared me to the owner. I was proud of myself. Now, I could afford a trip abroad without a man's help. It would not matter that I used the cheapest possible airline that did not fly directly to England. It was an unbelievable feat. Next, I took up the challenge of getting a foreign degree. I applied for a post graduate certificate in Education from a top British University. This was going to cost a little over three thousand pounds; a very big stride for me, yet I took it up. I bought a second taxi. Hard work pays, I never stopped reminding myself.

With my teaching job, my other side job, my schooling, oversight for my transport business and being a mother, my plate was

In and Out

considerably full. Asking for more would have been definitely overburdening and a breakdown was not negotiable. I trudged on.

In and Out

5

SWEETEST TABOO

Fourteen months after my pregnancy sojourn, he was completely locked up. Actually, we had stopped any form of make out by the seventh month. I thought it was because of the pregnancy. My tummy was copiously protuberant. It must have portended some sort of discomfort. I was great at finding excuses for my man. When I was loyal, I was loyal to the core. Many times, I made advances at him, he declined. Sometimes nicely, other times harshly. It was not necessarily that I enjoyed it from him. It was for the fact that a couple should indulge in it. I never had an orgasm (I found out about orgasm after our separation). Many times, in my quiet moments, I wondered what sex was all about. A few minutes of having penetration, the man makes his secretion and that was it! Yes, I loved the kissing and caressing but the actual coitus was not enthralling. I cared less about sex if there was no love. With love, we would kiss and have good foreplay. I lived a very religious and boring life. I spent most of my life in church where sexual matters were not openly discussed. I was not adventurous in that area either. By the time, Eka and I were no more; all that I thought of myself had to be redefined.

I had sex for the purpose of procreation and to satisfy my man. It was almost never about me. I do not remember any day he commended me for great sex. I do not recall him complaining either. We both tagged along probably pretending all was well.

The absence of it was beginning to get me worried.

35

In and Out

The first few months had what I would consider tenable excuses. The pregnancy terminated with a caesarian section. I had to heal. This was understandable. The second reason was that he witnessed the opening and the closing of the abdomen, the tear, the blood, the removal, the cleaning, the stitches, the catheter and every step involved from the theatre to the ward.

As soon as the doctor informed me that one of the babies was breached and that surgery was inevitable, I started planning for a covered delivery. I presented Eka with the option of being the video man or having the hospital do it for an extra fee. I preferred my darling husband to handle it. I thought seeing me go through birthing would make him love, respect and cherish me the more. I thought it would make our relationship unbreakable.   I was happy he accepted. On the other hand, Eka considered it a great privilege, not many women would give their husbands such an opportunity. I had no inclination that I was undoing myself. Was I undoing myself?

It was traumatic for him, so he alleged. For this, his third leg could not act, it refused to perform for a whole year and two months, for certainty, it didn't perform on me. Eka insisted that his pencil shaped tool was traumatized and perhaps needed counselling sessions. And our relationship was never the same.

From the seventh month to about the tenth month after birth, we had no sort of sexual activity even in my dream, yet we slept on the same bed. At that time, we lived in a two-bedroom flat. Guests and house-help stayed in one room. The rooms were not very big. By the time the twins were turning a year old, we moved to a three-bedroom spacious house and sex-deprivation continued for another four months. As I persisted, a drab coitus would happen once in a quarter and sometimes in six months. I would have endured it but for the fact that there were other women, not one, not two. My life was at risk! For more years, our relationship was devoid of real sex and romance. I was very sad especially the memories of it.

XXXXXXXXXXXXXXXXXXXXXXXXXXXXXXXXXXXXXXXXXXXXXXXXX

I preferred cleaning and tidying to cooking.

On this bright Saturday, I was about my routine. I moved from our room to the living room. I shared the same room with my husband. I thought it was right and romantic. Perhaps if I were to go the marriage path again, I may reconsider this option. It was the turn of the book shelf to experience my Midas touch. I was happy doing this as it brought back memories of all the books I savoured. Before the union got a better part of me, I read as wide as I could. I invested money in all sort of books. I dreamt about being an author someday.

While at it, I had a need to go into the bedroom which was adjacent the living room area that housed the bookshelf. I needed to change the cleaning water and the bedroom convenience was the closest. I went in, got fresh water and made for the door towards the shelf.

"Come here."

I knew it was him, he was lying down by the time I was making for the bathroom.

I stopped. I turned. He beckoned with his hand, "here", he said.

I went.

"Sit down."

37

In and Out

I sat.

"Lie down."

I laid.

"Open your legs."

I did.

The business was quickly finished save that it was not profitable in anyway, not in cash or otherwise.

xxxxxxxxxxxxxxxxxxxxxxxxxxxxxxxxxxxxxxxxxxxx

"Sweetheart, I noticed some rashes around my penis. I went to the pharmacy and was given some antibiotics. Can you do me a favour of checking yourself, take some drugs and make sure you are fine, too?"

This SMS must have been intended for his lover but was mistakenly sent to my phone. I laughed. I knew it. I needed no prophet to tell me he was up and about. While his nail like instrument was very active in other quarters, it would not work on me in months. I knew it could not have been me. More so, he never used that pet name with me. I understood the play. I never discussed this message beyond my reply, *'I got your message'*. I knew there was no need to make further ado. He would deny all the same.

That was the beginning of my complete emotional wreckage. I knew he was not a faithful husband. I had my instincts whisper to me. I could not concretise it. Even with the mistaken text message on my phone, I knew him, it was not proof enough. Funnily, I was never looking for proof. I did not bother sniffing. My focus was on myself, doing my part, being a good wife and mother. I left him to his

38

In and Out

conscience and to karma. One night, I stumbled on his new email address and the many conversations he had with his lovers.

Have you received the money? Pls check cos all the fx I did same day, they have gotten theirs. Ok? I love you babe.
Eka

my love,
for you on this valentine, I say to you make me happy and I love you dearly
I miss you
eky

Honey,
U r just beautiful. My aphrodisiac. I love you till death.
Eky

Honey, your email hurts. how can you even think of that talkless of concluding and saying bye to me in that manner? 'take care bye' communication is very important in any relationship.
I fainted on Friday early evening in my office, I was rushed to the hospital and it was my bp.
I was under intensive care till yesterday night. it's all loads of issues that are becoming too heavy for my heart. pls I can't be tired of you. and I can't leave you. pls don't drift away from me. that will kill me. unless you want me to leave a suicide note somewhere b4 that happens.
I found joy and happiness in you rita. i know your circumstances, but don't throw me away. pls be patient with me. i love you with all my heart.
pls I do.
Eky

Am gonna miss you too baby. I will call you ok? Pls if any cheque comes to the acct, pls pay. Try and disturb those guys for the money. Ok?
I hope to meet you real good. Try and let us get more closer pls.
I love you nnenna.
Am in lagos now waiting for my flight.
Bye for now and always try to send emails to me.
Eka

    Dumbfounded! Distraught! Disappointed! Disheartened! Destabilized! I was all five and more!

In and Out

Now, more than anything else, I was dealing with a serial cheat, a hardened criminal. How does this innocent looking man have the heart to be fooling so many ladies? How could he be such an expert? Eka's mien looked like he could not melt butter. He was always calm. It would take being very close to unravel his nuances.

A fateful night in the month of July, by the fifth year of our marriage, remains sour in my heart. Eka was done checking his email, he slept with the laptop still open and his email box not logged out. It was almost midnight. I took the laptop to check my mail. We had only one laptop. We took turns to use it. Eka went to work with it. It stayed with him till he slept. I was the last to go to bed. I used it for the rest of the night. I concluded my daily routine with checking my mail before sleeping off.

Turning the laptop to myself, I noticed a strange email box was open. The first email I noticed was a love note, then I saw several romantic mail exchanges from about five women. A particular Caucasian sent pictures of their escapades during his last China trip. I immediately had a clear understanding of the appearance of rashes round his penile area. A serial cheat has no taming! I forgave. He continued.

One day, in the seventh year of our marriage, I was off to work. I usually left early in order to drop the children at school. It was a Thursday and I had forgotten an important document at home. It was a few minutes before 9:00am. I figured I could drive down and back within a few minutes. I got home to meet Eka and his lover in our home. Even though I rattled them until the lady ran off, this became the sorest of the wounds. I hurriedly returned to work. At work, I was a shadow of myself. I wondered what to do with this idiot. In my eyes,

In and Out

he was one. Ultimately, I was grateful he was not touching me. I feared getting infected.

Again, I forgave. Life continued. He continued.

The days after our uncelebrated tenth marriage anniversary, things were irretrievably broken down. Our relationship was worse than two neighbours who did not see eye to eye. He hardly came home, and was not supporting the children and I financially. News had it that he'd rented a flat and cohabited with one of his ladies.

On a particular day, I went shopping in a choice supermarket. A soft-spoken, clean-looking gentleman who looked advanced in age saw me. He walked up to me like any man who beheld a damsel would. We seemed to have clicked immediately. I smiled. We exchanged numbers. Linus didn't live in that city, he simply visited. His impression made me look forward to seeing him again. We had no holds - barred discussions. Morning, noon or night, over the phone. He had time for me, and I for him.

It is dangerous to leave an adult lonely. He was soon due to visit the city. He let me in on his schedule. I opted to be his chauffeur from the airport. I dressed to kill in addition to being beautiful. I waited patiently at the airport for his arrival. I wondered how and what I would explain if Eka saw me. I brushed off my thoughts. He was not a saint. I was ready for the worst. Before this time, I already made up my mind to go for the kill. This was in June before I moved out in August. The recent events had forced me to start an exit plan. Linus was a tool in the plan. I became highly focused. Once I tuned off, I was off. I was no longer on Eka's frequency. Even if he saw me, it would have hastened the impending crash. For me, he that was down need fear a fall no more.

41

In and Out

We drove straight to the hotel and the deed was nicely done. It was pleasurable. I enjoyed it.

A church girl gone bad. A traditional wife finds life. Here was a phallus at my disposal, no more deprivation and no more returning to my vomit. For me, it was forward ever. We did it again and again. He gave me life. I became rejuvenated. We went to the movies together, sat in VIP corners and kissed ourselves out of this world. We went to exotic restaurants. I drove in his car. He gave me money too. I spent some nights with him howbeit cautiously. Love is life and life is good.

I tasted the forbidden fruit and concluded it was no taboo after all.

6

THE OVERRIDE

"Di, policemen are here to arrest me."

"What? Why? Give them the phone."

"Hello, officer. Good afternoon. My name is Dinaka Chima, my mum says you are in her house."

"Good afternoon, madam. I am Inspector Msugh. Yes, we are in her house."

"Is everything okay?"

"Erm, if everything was okay, we would not be here but we believe everything will be fine."

"So then, what brought you guys?"

"Well, there was a petition against her from Abuja. We are here to investigate."

"Interesting! What is the petition about please?"

"If you need to know, meet us at the station."

"I am in Abuja, it is not possible for me to meet you guys over there."

"It is in connection with some children's disappearance. We are investigating and will keep you posted."

43

"Alright then, please can you give the phone back to my mum? Thank you."

"Okay, madam."

"Mum, just do as they say, do not say what you don't know. I will keep in touch."

"Alright."

I could literally piece together what could have happened. Eka must have petitioned the police about the children. I took them with me as soon as my instincts completed a mental picture of his plot following the trajectory of his activities.

Eka was gradually moving out of the house. He had moved his wardrobe, the family document folder containing our marriage certificate, international passports, children's birth certificates, property documents, and more. He removed his workstation, his big coloured printer inclusive; flat screen television and he was no longer coming home every night. He stopped eating at home and no longer gave us feeding money. He blocked my phone from reaching him. When I tried with another line, it went through but from my phone, I could not get to his line. He kept sending false alarm of an alleged plot by me to poison him. I did not understand this mind game. Indeed, he took me unawares. Since December of the previous year, I could count the number of nights he had spent at home, not that he was out of town. It was already August.

One of the days, after another physically exasperating, demeaning and near-death bout, Eka disappeared as usual. I whisked the children off in the morning. I traveled as fast as lightning. No one knew I was on a journey of no return. For me, Eka just died. I took not

In and Out

more than three pairs of clothes for the children and for myself. There was no time to move anything else. Even if there was, I had nowhere to move them to. I could not bother moving them either because I wanted a quiet exit. He tipped the security guard to keep him abreast of my movement. I figured that a casual movement was the deal breaker.

At that time, I was jobless and had no money. My strength came from the premise of having life and the will to redeem it. This was the boldest decision I ever took. I gave myself a pat on the back.

"Hello, can I talk to my children?"

"You need to talk to me first."

"I am not interested in talking to you."

"Well then."

"I want to talk to my children."

"I have stated my position."

"Ok then, bye."

"Bye."

Eka was always on a very high horse. This was his phone call about a week later. I thought the two of us should have a discussion. I needed a closure. I hoped that when we talked, we would agree on the way forward especially with the children's welfare. Instead of a discussion, he preferred police brutality. It is only in Nigeria that a man would send the police after his mother-in-law to get his children knowing fully well that the children are with his wife. It is in Nigeria that the police will travel this distance without phone calls. The Nigerian elites had the police at their thumbs. Once money was

45

In and Out

flashed, reasoning was dumped. Eka's plan to intimidate and humiliate my entire clan with the police was not going to yield anything. He had threatened my elder brother and uncles from both my maternal and paternal sides. Was I perturbed? Not in the least. Besides being financially weak to join his fight, I knew that the best revenge was not to be immediate. We still have life ahead of us.

It was already three months since I had started my new job. I was doing well. I was at work when the phone call from my mum came through. I could not help but wonder how our police force functioned. What was the offence that needed the police to visit my home in the eastern part of the country from Abuja? I exuded uncommon courage and strength for a woman with my roughened history. Strength is more mental than physical. I was not intimidated. My colleagues did not know what was happening. As I followed through with the policemen, I was informed that my mum would be brought to Abuja from Uwani that night. This meant one thing only, an arrest and a detention. They said that "money talked, bullshit worked', nothing was truer in Nigeria.

A few months ago, I was at the police station to report domestic violence. The police taunted me. They did not believe my report. They said there were no marks or bruises of any sort to support my allegation.

"Madam, if it was just a slap, you need to learn to stay out of your husband's way then" the police lady advised.

"He beat me, he tried to strangle me" I responded

"But there are no marks to show. Do you have any injury?"

"I don't understand you, ma'am"

In and Out

"I mean, for you to claim you were beaten, there has to be blood or marks or perhaps a red eye. You look normal. Where is the evidence of physical abuse? Do you have any doctor's report?" The police lady continued.

I was dumbfounded.

"Can I make my report?" I enquired

"No madam, this is family matters. We do not open files for such things. I advise you to go home, stay out of his way. If he beats you to stupor, that is the only time we can come in. For now, there is no evidence of assault".

I went home with my heads bowed. I felt so defeated and powerless.

This disappointment from the police made me weary. If I was rich or 'highly connected' as defined in our clime; I would have surely been served better. Thinking of my mum, I was very certain that they embarked on another oppressive venture.

After work, I made a series of calls. I needed help. I was unsure of the real nature of the petition and how much money would be involved. Nigeria had never been a fair country. The rich ruffled the poor using the police. They won most cases. Again, bail was not as free as we were made to believe.

"Good evening, mama. I hope you are all well. So, you and your son arrested my mother?" I said to Eka's mother on the phone.

"Well, you took our children. Eka would have to do anything he can to get back his children."

In and Out

"Did I hear you right? Eka is arresting my mother and this is all you are saying?"

"But I asked you to bring the children, you refused. Where are they? Bring them out."

"Which children? My own children? I am short of words. You people are starting a war. We shall see how it ends."

I cut the conversation with Eka's mother. Nne swung from left to right. I was no longer confused with her position. Since the year before when Eka activated his missing-in-action mode, Nne feigned ignorance each time I called to report. She would say "come home with the children, come and tell us what happened." I never really understood her statement to mean support for Eka. She took it with a pinch of salt. By April, I got miffed with her continuous request for the children to be brought to the village. "Mama, why are you insisting on bringing the children? I told you that your son has left the house. I told you how he beats me. I told you all that was happening and all you have to say is bring the children. Do you have any problem with the children?"

"It is when you come home with the children that we will be able to listen to your complaints. This is not a phone conversation. You must come home and you must come along with the children."

I could sense the plot. I was not to be fooled again.

I had kept my mum in the dark concerning my home affairs all the while. The sly tone of my mother-in-law left me no option than to get my mum involved. My mum listened patiently to the long conversation. She was shocked that I hadn't told her any of this till now. She wondered what could be done then swung into action immediately.

My mother, Eyi, called Eka as soon as she got off the phone with me. According to her report back to me, Eka was adamant and informed her outright that he was done with the marriage. She called Nne to go to Abuja and sort things out. Nne declined on the excuse that her husband was sick and she was looking after him. Nne rather suggested that I came with the children. Eyi was worried about her stance. She asked me not to move an inch. She told me to make sure that the children never left my sight for a minute. Eka and his family were together in this, and they were up to no good, so I believed.

A day in October, Nne went to Visit Eyi in Uwani. She went with food stuff. According to Eyi, she brought food for her grandchildren. Eyi did not hide her displeasure. "Do you suppose that if the children were with me, they would be hunger smitten? I begged you to go to Abuja and help our children reconcile, you refused and now you are in my house to talk about grandchildren. Where is my daughter? Where is the daughter I gave you people to marry?" There was no concordance between them. The grandchildren were not even in Eyi's house. They had never visited her. The last time she saw them, they were barely a month old. Whatever gave the Chimas the impression that the twins were in Uwani was unknown. Nne apparently left without seeing them. She believed they were hidden. According to Eyi, Nne was not on a reconciliation mission. She came to spy. Her foodstuff was rejected. There was a deadlock. The die was cast!

The police arrived with my mum to Abuja about midnight and asked me to meet them at the station. I was wise enough not to go. I would have been detained as well. It was a Friday night. Eka's plan was to have both of us detained so that he would elope with the

In and Out

children. No woman is as daft as she may seem. How could he think so lowly of my entire family? Did he suppose we were that brainless not to match his action with wise reactions? I kept mussing within me. It was Friday, December 18th.

The next day was a Saturday. I got to the police station in the company of my friend, Maggie. I was shown the petition. '… while I was away, Dinaka Ezenna made away with my kids. …they were sighted hawking on the streets of Lagos. Efforts to rescue them proved abortive. They were recently sighted in the city of Uwani malnourished and street hawking. The lady in collaboration with her mum, Ifeadi Ezenna …' the bottom line is that the two women mentioned were being accused of child labour, child trafficking, child molestation and child abuse. The children in question were mine. How does it make sense that a husband and a father in agreement with his lawyer pulled this sort of stunt? What sort of investigation would make the Nigerian Police Force deploy resources to Uwani to effect an arrest without involving the principal suspect ……… me? Laughable indeed!

I was no longer Dinaka Ezenna. I had become Dinaka Chima. I had a change of name done few months after our marriage, why was he using my maiden name? This was another show of his crookedness. I was not perturbed.

Eka definitely crossed the boundary with his display of prowess and influence. He desecrated the '*ogo*' relationship. How could he have his mother -in-law detained over her grandchildren? Ironically, the woman was innocent. The last time she saw those children was ten years earlier.

The next morning, I arrived at the police office with the children. I shielded them from saying a word to their father. First, I did

In and Out

not want them divulging any information on their whereabouts and second, they were my negotiating tool. Everything we toiled for, Eka took with him. I took the children. I felt this was just fair. Besides, was I going to leave my children for his mistresses to raise? After the preliminary interrogation by the police department, instead of having this false alarmist duly punished, they simply chided him. They asked him to go to court if he wanted custody. I was allowed to leave with the children. With all his money and influence, a simple woman overturned him once again. He definitely could not explain how this was possible in Nigeria. Strength is not always in numbers.

In and Out

7

ONE ACCUSATION, TOO MANY

11:15pm, Easter Monday. She tiptoed quietly into the room as I directed. There was a mixture of hunger and anger. Someone had just put on a daredevil cap.

I had been chatting with her for over 3 hours. We talked about everything; past, present and future. We were just getting to know each other and were fascinated by how much divergent we were and the few salient similarities. I narrowed on the similarities. I was roused.

"What if I asked you to come?" I inquired from my chat buddie.

"I will."

"Then come."

It was already past midnight yet this invitation was honoured. For one it was the first, for another, it was the practice. I quickly opened the guest room and had her wait for me. Everywhere was still. I joined her in the room and in the bed. I was determined. I touched her upper body and she touched back. We looked each other in the eyes. There was a mutual consensus and we continued. To me, it was the most pleasurable activity ever. This was not just new but savoury. We did not want it to stop. Stolen meat is always the sweetest.

The night continued peacefully, satisfaction was depicted with a broad grin as I laid to sleep. I had just visited a new world without a

52

In and Out

visa. "I would try this again. I needed to do all there is to do about it", I told myself as I dozed off.

So, we began our unusual friendship. We were no longer just chat buddies but full-blown sexual partners. We met whenever opportunity allowed, we waxed strong. Life abhors any vacuum.

Eka soon became curious about my radiance. I was no more sulking. I was happy and flaunted it. I paid attention to my looks more. My partner wanted it so. She took me shopping and from her not too full purse, she made sure I was comfy first. He became jealous but could not pin it to anything. He knew my partner. Her hubby is his friend. I was sure his little mind could not have suspected any foul play else he would have flown off the handle! Sometimes Eka quizzed his friend about us but got no information. Nma's husband did not care. He was cool with us. Everyone and everything is useful in more than one way.

"How long have you been at this?" I inquired.

"This is my life", she replied.

"Does he know?"

"I doubt if he knows. He simply knows I don't like doing it with him."

"Then why did you marry him?"

"Well, pressure … we did it once, I got pregnant and umm, we married."

"I never knew I had the tendency."

"Every woman has."

53

In and Out

"Really?"

"Sure, most women are bisexuals. I am talking from experience. You are just a good girl."

"Hmmm."

"He doesn't deserve you. Allow me to spoil you, please."

"My conscience says this is not right."

"What makes it wrong?"

"Isn't it cheating?"

"Nope and even if it is, it is allowed. I am not a man. I will give him his space."

"What did I get myself into?"

"Don't be too hard on yourself. He caused it. He left you. He doesn't care about you. There should be no vacuum anywhere."

"I'm not sure I can continue this."

"Please, don't let this stop. What we have is beautiful, you like the way I touch you, don't you?"

"Yes, but …"

"No buts, just enjoy it."

"And if we are caught?"

"Till then. For now, let's live one day at a time."

It no longer mattered whether he slept at home or not. He had stopped sleeping at home for a while. Eka and I were co-tenants from

In and Out

the way we lived. He came home some mornings to change his clothes. He had blocked me from reaching him on the phone. When Eka came home, he would not even answer my greeting nor eat my food. We lived as independent as possible. I had stopped caring. I was in another world. Does every human not have the capacity to be both good and bad?

I was a fervent member of my local church. I loved God and did my best with service to humanity too. I saw myself as a preacher. Indeed, I led a lot of church activities. I was considered a role model in my church.

The news about my disagreement with my husband was soon broken to the church leaders. They were asked to pray for me while I was relieved of all responsibilities. "You need to channel all your energy towards making your relationship with your husband work", my pastor told me. "You will no longer lead the leaders and work in the church office. For now, we need you to be emotionally stable. Fix your home. May God give you peace." I assumed the leaders kept me in their prayers. I was generally loved and I knew it.

As a Christian, I reported my lesbian activities to my pastor. My conscience knew it was wrong and I could not continue. I turned myself in. I was prayed with, after days of fasting. I would not head the leadership council anymore. I willingly let go of any other church responsibilities too. I paused church as I began to question the essence of life. I was not prepared for the snowball of emotional trauma. I was completely down and help was not in sight.

"Your husband said you were involved with your pastor."

55

"I learnt you were frolicking with other men."

"Hmmm, he told me you moved out of the house."

"Eka said you quit the marriage."

"Madam, you are a very ungrateful woman, is it not the man that sent you and your children abroad? What harm could he possibly do to you to make you quit your marriage?"

"I heard you quit your well-paying job for a church secretary?"

"He said you wanted to poison him so he stopped eating your food, how could you?

"He said that the day you insisted on working against his wish was the day the marriage ended."

"He said you refused to cook for the children, you prefer to hire a cook."

"He said you are very lazy and very materialistic and you don't want to work."

"He said you are dating an army general and you had lunch at the Hilton Hotel with him?"

"He said you don't respect him and you don't want to be controlled"

There were too many voices, too many questions, too many accusations. These voices did not come to seek the truth, they came with more condemnation. They had taken sides with him without knowing me. To some, he showed messages taken out of context while to others, he fabricated lies that were sweet to the ears.

56

In and Out

"What else does callous mean?" I thought rigorously. I was utterly dismayed. I summoned courage to put the bits together; they were not necessarily adding up. There was no fracas or major disagreement before he started taking his things out of our home. I had never been this confused. While grappling with this perniciousness, another attack was launched at me. There was a phone call. It was the voice of a lady. She did not say beyond 'hello'. I believed she did this for me to know that she was a lady. She started sending her missiles in the form of text messages to my phone.

Slim witch...pastor's girlfriend, even the bible says wife be submissive, not seen your kind of maggot before, u think u are smart but you are the dumbest. Be warned. When am ready 4 u, that church will be shut down

Watch your back stupid wicked woman. I know you won't reply but am ready 4 your dumb ass

I tot you are a tigress, why aren't you taking my calls? Well will soon come harass you in that your stupid church where all ur pastor does is breaking homes. Stupid barren bastard.

She sent three messages consecutively. I ransacked my memory trying to put a name or face to the texts. Could it be the girl who was used as his Profile Picture on WhatsApp messenger? Could it be the one he recently travelled to Dubai with? Perhaps she is the one he is living with. What would have given her the effrontery to fight me? Did I get in her way? There were no answers. I should not add this to my baggage. I should not be bothered by a faceless fool. "Did you just refer to her as a faceless fool?" I asked myself. "Of course, she is! What sort of a girl uses such gutter approach?" I convinced myself. Whoever this lowlife lover was, she was not worth replying. I was too polished for such guerilla warfare. For one, she could not face me neither could she speak correctly. I had one conclusion; Eka is a fool and does not deserve me. I would be very glad to walk away. I had endured loads of brutality from him. What more was I in the marriage for? I knew that technically the marriage was non-existent.

57

In and Out

Unfortunately, just like contracting a marriage involved families, legalities and sometimes ceremonies, dissolution followed same. For our case, we had a statutory one, walking out does not just end it. I had my fears.

I took up the job of a church administrative assistant after quitting from my school job. My main consideration was my love for God first and then the fact that the church office was more flexible. It would allow my sufficient period to optimally perform my family duties. The church office was also closer to home. Eka did not want a working wife so it would not matter if I worked in school or church. My pay for being an administrative assistant was half of the school's. I was to resume at 9:00am against 7:00am at the school and could close at 4:00pm on non-service days as against closing at 5:00pm. I had a full hour's break to myself for school pick-up as against fifteen minutes. To me, the church work was friendlier and suited my need to keep both family and my service to God working. The church office was closer to both home and the children's school. It was more centrally located than the school which was at one end of the city. I prayed to God, "If this church work is your will for me Lord, please convince my husband." I settled for the church work. Eka was displeased; he neither shared it with me nor showed it. I figured this out as the questions poured in. What will be usually becomes.

I gave my best, it was not good enough. I withdrew my best. I encouraged myself and moved on with life, this time, I took it slow with everything about church and God. Meeting Linus was one of the turning points for me. I knew I wasn't ever going back to Eka again.

In and Out

8

PEACE IN PIECES

One beautiful Monday afternoon, Eka's younger sister, Asumpta sent a message to me; *'Auntie, I will be coming back on Wednesday'*.

She had been living with Eka before I came into his life. She was about twelve or thirteen years old, beautiful, intelligent and cooperative. Usually, in-laws gave a lot of trouble. It was an unfortunate reflex behaviour that most ladies here encountered in their marriage journey. I think I was very lucky not to have faced lots of difficulties from my husband's immediate family. I thought they liked me until events started unfolding. We got by. Their animosities were not expressed openly at me. Eka had six siblings, one was my favourite, another was too occupied with his evangelistic work, and he never bothered me. I managed to get along with his two sisters. I knew I was a constant object of discussion. I knew because my favourite tipped me off. He too was considered a black sheep of the family. His mother gave off smiles and pretended all was well.

Asumpta became a boarder after her Junior Secondary School. She was happy to be in the boarding house. My mum helped work it out in her city. Everybody was happy that Asumpta was off to a very good school. She was to return to our home every holiday. Asumpta however, preferred to visit her parents in the village each holiday. This was how she stayed away from our house and only came on special occasions. Soon, three years were over and she was done with secondary school. Eka helped her get into a university in Bauchi State. Between finishing secondary school and getting to the university, she visited whenever she wanted. Her university was closer home than to

59

In and Out

Ekwulobia where her parents lived so she also spent her holidays with me. She was careful to inform me whenever she wanted to come. She was faring well. '*Your brother no longer stays here. He moved out. Please find out where he is and stay with him*', I responded to her message.

I mustered enough courage to send such a response. At that point, I was no longer safe and I knew it. My instincts were all I had. I believed Eka could suddenly whisk the children away or even do something brash. I was relentlessly uneasy; mindful of whom I opened my door to. I knew my refusal was likely to fan another war. I had thrown all caution to the wind at this point considering that the marriage had technically given way. For me, the sudden realization that it was over, hardened my heart. I was done with crying and begging and submitting.

Eka's personal effects were not in the house anymore. I did not know what stunt he planned next. The rent had expired since February and this was August. I suspected that he would aim for the children. I swore by my life to keep them. Removing things could be easier but certainly moving two children would not be without a huge fight, that is if I had any inclination of his modus operandi.

I had forgotten about my discussion with Asumpta. I carried on with my daily schedule. The children were on holiday. I feared leaving them by themselves hence I was stuck at home looking after them and facing other home chores. No sooner had I relaxed in my room that Wednesday evening than I heard shouts of excitement from the children. My room was the farthest from the house entrance. I walked briskly to the door. My children had opened the door, allowing both Eka and Asumpta in.

60

On seeing both, I was greatly displeased. I would not have this, not anymore. I had nothing more to fear anyway. Asumpta was in the guest room about to settle in. I had to speak. I just had to speak to her.

"Girl, you have always come here, I have always opened my door to you. I insist this time that you will not be here and I mean it. Your brother no longer stays here and I will not have it any other way."

I warned her firmly and walked back to my room. Few minutes later, Eka walked into the room obviously furious.

"What did you say to Asumpta?"

"I meant what I said."
"This is my house. I paid for it, I call the shots."

"I meant what I said."

"Well, if anyone will leave, it will be you. She is my sister, she stays."

"You are here to fight me as usual? Ok, fight me", I pushed him.

The grand fight began. This was the mother of all fights we ever had. I fought back. I tried to return every slap, every punch and every nasty word. I did not fully succeed. He was heavier than me. He had always been uncouth. He had lived on the streets. He knew how to fight, I didn't. I was not his match in anyway. I wished I was. I used my teeth, my nails. I was no longer to be the victim. We were both going to tell the story. I fought with all my might. When my strength began to wane, I went downstairs and vented my anger on his car. I smashed his windscreen. I sat down by the stairs and wept like a baby. It was all over. I mourned, I grieved, I cried like never before. To me, I just failed woefully, I was a failure. The ten-year-old journey came flashing back. What were the memories of this sojourn? What could I

61

hold on to? As I continued crying, I heard footsteps. I looked up and behold Eka with his sister and the children about to leave.

I roared, "Not on your life will you cross this gate with my children, not while I'm alive! Guys, (looking towards my children), come this way". The troubled children soon moved to my side. They obviously did not want a monstrous man for a father. A man that beats their mum was not a dad. They seemed to be on my side. My son moved to me without batting an eyelid. My daughter followed closely. They were both undoubtedly embarrassed. The whole neighbourhood stood still for Eka and me. This was the first time our uncivilized behavior was in public glare. One can only imagine what was going on in everyone's mind.

Indeed, Kamsi and Nasa had witnessed several fights between us. Once, I went for school pick-up. When I got to the class and greeted Kamsi's teacher as my manner was, she was very cold to me. I halted.

"Is everything okay? How did my son fare today?"

"Um, um", she began to stutter and scratch her head.

"Is anything the matter?"

"Kamsi did not talk to anyone today. He did not do anything today."
"How do you mean? Is he alright?

"Please come and sit down."

"I hope all is well. Where is he?"

"He is over there."

In and Out

I looked over, and saw my son looking well but he seemed very quiet. I wondered what the problem could be. The suspense was beginning to get to me.

"Talk to me, please. What's wrong?"

"We all kept wondering. He refused to talk, to write, to participate in anything at all. We even got his sister to talk to him. He was moody all through the day. I called my colleague to help me. Everyone that tried could not get Kamsi to speak …"

"So?" I cut in. "I will talk to him". I turned to her son, "Darling, where is your sister? Get her and let's go." The boy looked morose. This was definitely not my son. "Are you alright, sweet? What happened? Will you tell me, please?" I asked him.

Kamsi was in year 3, a seven-year-old. He was usually a quiet child. He bottled up a lot. He hardly complained even as a baby. I always wondered how he learnt to endure. I paid more attention to him than his sister. His countenance, his body movement, his eyes, his smile, his nod, everything was literally interpreted. Most times, I was right. For both sadness and excitement, Kamsi rarely showed it.

"Excuse me, madam. We took him to the headteacher when we didn't succeed", said Ms. Panto.

"And …"

"Please calm down, madam."

"How am I supposed to be calm? Speak!" I snapped.

"It's just that sometimes, you don't know the best way to convey a message."

In and Out

"My dear, go on and say it any way you want", my temper was rising!

"Kamsi said he saw his daddy trying to strangle his mummy last night …"

"Oh, my goodness!" I cut in. "Oh dear, not again. He was quiet all through the day, right? Did he eat? Did he write? Did he talk? Did he even play?" I queried

"He has been a shadow of himself all day, he barely did anything today. I …"

"I am so sorry, very sorry you had to deal with this. I will take care of it; I will surely take care of it, please. I am sorry. Yes, his father beat me. He saw us. I am ashamed, very ashamed. I apologise. Oh, my goodness, oh dear …"

I was highly embarrassed. I took my children from the class to my car, flabbergasted; I kept apologizing to them as we drove home.

Again, this child was witnessing another episode of violence against his mother. This was enough reason to end the marriage. It held nothing for my son or any of us anyway. Eka was a serial cheat. He was a liar; he was a domestic violent bandit. What was good about him? He was controlling, manipulative, intimidating, wicked, uncaring and irresponsible. There was nothing good to be associated with him. Maybe there was, but in my circumstance, I could not think of any or perhaps the bad outweighed the good. Fury had overtaken my sense of reasoning. This once cherished husband had become the devil's twin. I had enough memories to keep me raging.

In and Out

He left the premises without the children. Asumpta went with him. I went upstairs crying uncontrollably. Unhappiness was my lot. I was ashamed of myself. I had no more dignity, without a doubt, we were done. There was nothing to hold onto anymore. The marriage was a sham. I cursed Eka from the depths of my soul. I did not spare myself either. I hated myself for the many years I'd endured his bullying, for staying so long, for covering him up. I gave my cheek a resounding slap, then another one. "You are a fool", I soliloquized. Then both hands kept going back and forth on my cheeks as I lambasted myself. This was the first time I was hitting myself this much. My eyes were filled with rage. How could I allow a man born of a woman deal me such hard blows? I could not swallow this hard pill. I wept hopelessly; there was no one to console me. Sleep took over. The children were already asleep, it was almost midnight.

It was soon dawn and I woke up. I'd barely slept. My braids were littered all over the room with my hair attached to them. During the previous day's fight, Eka had fun pulling off my hair. He beat me mercilessly. I was feeling pain all over my body as I woke up. I gathered the braids into a polythene bag. I had an early shower. I planned to be at a couple of places. It was a busy day for me. I got the children ready too. The idea of looking prim and proper was not on the table. It didn't matter what anyone looked like. I had limited time to accomplish my plans.

As soon as the children had eaten breakfast, I made for my car key. I looked everywhere for it and did not find it. Then I looked at the parking lot, my car was not there. I already knew who took it. I laughed at myself again. "For how long would this man be ahead of you?" I queried. "Well then, since he wants all the properties of the marriage, he can have them." I shrugged this off and went for a taxi.

65

In and Out

The fear of the unknown made me keep the children in a friend's house. That way, I was sure of their whereabouts. I ran my errands including a visit to the police station to report domestic violence and car theft.

"Madam, this is a family issue", said the police woman.

"How is this a family issue, madam?" I responded

"What do you want us to do?"

"Are you asking me?"

"You will not write any statement, this is a family issue. We will call your husband and talk with him."

"Really?"

"Give us his name and number."

"His name is Eka Chima, his number is 080…..3."

"Ok."

"What next, madam?"

"Wait, I will call him right away so that we can fix a meeting time."

"Ok then."

She dialed the number; a meeting was scheduled for 10:00am the next day. The next day, Eka showed up in the company of his lawyer and friends. I had just a clerk from Barrister Martin's office with me. It was another show of power. Eka is naturally ostentatious. He knew how to show off. We were called into the DPO's office. Mr Bello listened as Eka bragged about all the supposedly great things he had done for me and my siblings. He also boasted of how he took care of the children and me, from having vacations abroad to using an expensive phone, to driving an expensive car, Eka exaggerated as much as he could. For me, it was not a time for elongated discussion. My mind was made up; this husband is a fool of the highest order. "Who counts the food he gives to his family as a favour?" I pondered.

As was expected, Mr Bello made the final remarks: "The Nigerian law is in favour of women in matters like this. It is unfortunate that women do not take advantage of it because of our custom. Go home and settle and if you cannot, go to court." He dismissed everyone seeing that there was no head way. Eka denied being in a fight with me. He maintained that the car was his even though it was registered in my name. Just like me, he saw no good in me too. His narration of events left little to be desired of me. I guess we both had had enough. We should not have allowed this degree of deterioration. At this point, I could say my heart was black; it was very bitter towards my dear husband. His was probably blacker. He brandished his communication thread with his dad to Mr Bello. "Sir, see, this is my father's position concerning her. I should have sent her away a long time ago." Eka said as he handed over his mobile phone to him. "Do you know that this woman planned to poison me and the children? She has to go. We're no more interested in marrying her". He was reinforcing the decision his family made to send me away. It was my first time of hearing this. The picture was getting clearer. "As I said, sir, if you no longer want the marriage, please go to court. Our job is to broker peace and avoid violence and loss of lives. Please do not beat her again. Send her away if you cannot agree". Mr Bello concluded. Everyone left.

"This experience at the police station felt better. Mr Bello seemed a bit balanced" I consoled myself. I could not help but marvel

In and Out

at the phrase "send her away". Hearing of the consensus to send me away was both heart wrenching and heartwarming.

I went home. I changed the entrance padlock. I needed to secure my children. I invited Nyere to spend the night with me. Nyere was always in the know. She looked after the children as I played my sneaky games with Linus. By the first cock crow, I got the children ready and we left the city of Abuja. I took my handbag and the children's tablet computer and three sets of clothes for each of them. Nyere loaned me some money. I took some too from my neighbour, Oge. We were the first to arrive the bus park. I remained uneasy until the bus departed the park.

68

In and Out

9

UNREAD SIGNS

"I just got a call from the University, I got the admission", the excitement I had was overwhelming!

"What admission are you talking about?"

"The University of course, did we not go there together to submit the form for a post graduate course?"

"You will not go ooo. I did not marry you to go to school", Eka said warily.

This was about a month or two after our traditional marriage. Anyone within my radar at that time would testify that the only ambition I had was to have a PhD. I considered myself an intellectual. I found this passion for knowledge much later in life and was determined to follow through. My heartbeat was to get back to school even if it meant starting afresh. For one, I was not proud of the course I studied and the school I finished from.

I remembered the lovely afternoon. I had taken time off work for this purpose. I was still single. I lived in my house and had a fairly good job. It was a few months before I started dating Eka. He behaved really civil and offered help at any slightest chance. I mentioned my intention to submit my application form to the university, he offered to drive me. We planned the day and time. He kept to his word.

Eka picked me up from my office. He drove. For me, it was picturesque. I was usually swept off by very tender actions. I was that soft-hearted! We talked about the future and all other things lovers discuss. Our future looked bright. I was very happy. Soon, we arrived at the University, completed all necessary procedures and submitted my application for a post graduate course. I exchanged phone numbers with the relevant contacts and we began the drive back to town. The University was on the outskirts of the city.

69

"How lucky I was!" I thought to myself. My dream was a step closer. I was on my way to starting a master's degree programme.

Some weeks later, about a month or two into the marriage, there was a call from the University. I'd made the list of successful students, but alas …. This picture flashed back in my mind and without minding my tone, I reacted.

"How do you mean I will not go to school? Did you not take me to submit the form? What are you talking about?" I asked my husband. "All I know is that I did not marry you to go to school. I don't even have money to fund it anyway", he blurted. There was no form of empathy from him. How could this be? How could I be fooled this way? Who was messing with my brain? I kept quizzing myself with no answer. I was devasted. Two blows at near intervals - first was that he did not want a working, money-earning wife and now this.

This was one of the pointers. I should have probably been decisive on what I wanted with my life. He won again. I was unsure about my life's direction at twenty-seven years of age. On the one hand, I hoped to be the best of wives and on the other hand, I felt very strong about being an opinion leader. In my part of the world, both rarely go hand in hand considering that a good wife is measured by her submissiveness to her husband. The man is the only one to validate this aspect of her. What she thought of herself would not count if her man did not attest. At least, this was what I was brought up to think.

I was working with a computer company when I met Eka. He came with a friend of his for enquiries. I was the sales contact that attended to their queries. We exchanged business cards as professionals would do. He was in a similar line of business. Our business discussions became stretched and love happened. Less than a year of meeting, I lost my job with the computer company. The job came with a small apartment so I lost that too. I was given four days to vacate. Eka's house became the closest alternative. He lived in a slum on the outskirts of town. For me, this was a temporal act. I was very

In and Out

happy and grateful that he offered to share his home with me impromptu. I brought in all my stuff. I unknowingly landed in Eka's fishing net. I met Asumpta in his house.

It was a one-bedroom apartment with a small toilet, bath and a kitchenette. The property was sufficiently habitable unlike the surrounding buildings. The roads were earthen and had been plagued by erosion. It was a nightmare for car owners. This house was offered to Eka as soon as his first wife sent him packing. Mary was a lawyer from a comfortable home. She probably set Eka up because at the end of their marriage, he had absolutely nothing with him. He turned a new leaf with me by his side. A close friend owned the house that was eventually demolished by the Government as an illegal construction. The details of their separation were not very clear to me. This was another blunder. I should not have ignored this pertinent sign. I believe that his experience with Mary led to opposing more education and work by a woman.

There was peace either because a poor man is a humble man or because there was love between us.

The only window of the room opened to a 'shit area'. Most of the houses had no toilets. Many of the villagers resorted to 'bush balling'. There were two kinds of bush balling; one was to go straight in the safer area of the uncultivated bushy area of the environment and defecate. A safe area was rather free from snakes and all forms of dangerous creepy crawlies. The alternative was to discharge the waste matter in a polythene. It was thrown farther into the bush. This 'ball' could land anywhere depending on who flung it – the bush, the roof of thatched houses, the window of nearby houses and more.

Luckily, one could navigate through the bedroom and the living room. Asumpta slept in the living room while we used the bedroom. The only wooden piece of furniture in the house was the table my small cooker rested on. Eka moved in with his clothes only. The linoleum floor covering and the plastic chair were bought by both of

In and Out

us. There was a flushable toilet albeit no water supply. Water was bought from hawkers at a reasonable rate. Love makes a cave feel like a palace.

Asumpta and I got along quite well until one certain midday Saturday. Eka had gone off for the day's hustle. I was to go to the market. I was getting ready. I noticed that Asumpta was getting ready too. Asumpta was about twelve or thirteen years, she usually stayed at home after school or during the holidays. I pampered her as much as I could. She came back to school to meet her lunch and she did not prepare dinner. I took charge of the home like a typical wife and mother. As soon as I was ready and about to leave, I bid her good bye.

"Asumpta, please stay safe, I'm off to the market, I won't be long", I said as I made my way to the exit.

"Wait Auntie, I'm leaving with you."

"Sorry."

"I'm going with you. Brother said I should never allow you leave home alone."

"Meaning?"

"He doesn't want anyone to bother you on the road. He said if he wasn't with you, then I should be with you."

"You definitely can't be serious."

"I am. I must go with you else he will beat me."

"As my body guard?' Is it you that will be my body guard? How much protection can you give me?" I found this amusing.

"He said I should tell him everything you do, everything that happens when he is away."

In and Out

"Interesting!'' ''Alright then.' You aren't going with me. Sit your butt at home and read your books." I became firm.

I fumed and headed towards the gate. As soon as I got to the gate, I turned back to see Asumpta on my trail.

"What? Where are you off to?"

"Auntie, I don't want brother to beat me. I must follow you."

I angrily went back to the apartment, undressed and slept off. It meant there would be neither lunch nor dinner. Yet I stayed.

After a few months of being a live-in, I began to think of getting back to work. I picked my phone and sent an SOS message to all those I considered helpful in my contact. Fortunately, I got a reply from a former colleague. *'Go to No 51 Sege Street, Wuse 2, tomorrow, 9:00am, a new telecoms company is hiring, you may be lucky'*. I was excited. Going for the interview was not negotiable. The few months I stayed at his beck and call were the most horrible. He controlled me ruthlessly. I thought that getting a job would make things better for me.

Karmo was the name of the area we lived. It was highly under developed and distant from the city centre. The traffic was exhausting in the mornings as folks went to work. It was either one left before 6:00am or got caught in the traffic. Eka's electrical shop was located in Wuse 2, a highbrow area of the city. It should not be difficult to locate the address, I assured myself. We both left for the shop in his rickety car every morning while Asumpta resumed at her school. Out of boredom, I helped with sales and general business management. Eka was not that gifted with business management from what I saw. It was a sizeable shop but the stock was meagre. Most often, Eka depended on what was called *'oso ahia'* to survive. *Oso ahia* meant picking an

In and Out

item from another shop for a customer. Immediately the sale was made, the item was paid for. The profit was usually minimal except for rare cases where a customer was totally oblivious of the item's variables. There were trickles of government contracts too. Generally, Eka managed to stay afloat financially.

The night before, I intimated my man of my intending job hunt. He promised to find the address and drop me right at the venue. I believed him.

True to his words, Eka dropped me right in front of the location. It was easy to find. I got out of the car and thanked him. I was very confident of the position. I considered myself smart looking, ambitious, convincing, intelligent, self-motivating, persuasive and with requisite educational background and experience. After adjusting my dress, I turned to wave at Eka whom I believed should have reversed to take off. Surprisingly, he pulled over and was out of the car heading towards me.

"Is anything the matter my love?" I asked gently.

"No, not really. I wanted to take a peek into the premises and also to be sure it was the actual place you were headed. You can see there is no signage, nothing to show this is an office."

"Alright then, thanks for the care. So, are you going back as soon as I get in?"

"Certainly. I will stand and watch you get in before I drive off or would you rather I wait for you?"

"Erm, I'm not sure there is any need. Besides, we don't know how long it would take."

"Ok. See you later and best of luck."

"Thank you, my love."

I proceeded to the entrance. It was a fancy gate which you couldn't see through. I made it past the security checks. The environment spelt serenity. I continued to the reception area. The front desk officer was an amiable lady. After a brief interaction, I was ushered into the waiting area. There were other prospective employees. I bowed my head briefly to pray. Then I raised it and looked around to salute the people I met. I was shocked at whom I saw.

"What? You followed me? You said you were leaving, what exactly is the matter?" I maintained my calmness as I questioned.

"You are asking too many questions. I asked the security man, he said there were not many people so I decided to wait for you. Would you not rather I take you back? Besides, I am not sure your excitement allowed you to take your transport fare."

"Hmmm." there was a heavy sigh of relief from me. I did not believe him. I became worried and interpreted this as a bad omen. I sat quietly and ruminated over his response. I remembered the mini drama with Asumpta and the market. Eka and his sister have been policing me. He checked my phone while I slept. He never allowed me have cash at any time. The only time he gave me money was for grocery shopping and it had to be with his sister. "This is not just adding up", I muttered. "Will he also follow me to the board room where the interview held?" I was on edge. I was clearly losing my composure, my radiance and my enthusiasm. I looked at him. He would not let our eyes meet. I hoped for assurance from him but I did not get it. We were in a public place, I came for a job interview, I knew that raising my voice or any

In and Out

form of drama was a huge disservice to my aspirations. I remained calm, calm indeed!

It was soon my turn. I headed towards the boardroom. I crossed the first aisle and took a turn to the door. Just before I touched the hinge, I felt uneasy, I looked up and looked back. Eka was a few steps behind. Immediately he saw me lift my head, he turned as if he was returning to the waiting area. I heaved a sigh of relief. I knocked, opened and entered. I was fully persuaded that Eka will pull a stunt but unsure of what direction he would come from.

"Make yourself comfortable and introduce yourself, please."

"Thank you, sir", I responded with a smile and sat. It was a one-man panel.

"My name is Michael Uzo, the CEO of Hydra Communications…" He briefly said the company's vision and mission. He returned from the USA with a passion to improve communication in Nigeria. He was looking to recruit a passionate team that would help his vision materialize. As he talked, there was a knock on the door. He obliged and the door was opened. The door was behind me, I could only tell from his expression that whoever entered was uninvited. He was staring at the door for a few seconds. I held myself from looking back. My intention was to put up the best behavior and ultimately scale through this hurdle. If I got the job, I would leave Eka's house. I will be able to fend for myself.

"How may I help you?" Mr Michael asked.

"Erm, she, she …" I recognized his voice immediately. It was Eka. I became stifled at once. "She is my wife. Please, can I come in?" he

In and Out

asked. I was hoping he would be turned down. "Sure, come right in", retorted Mr Michael.

The interview continued but the atmosphere was no longer the same. There were a few questions and answers before the CEO thanked us for coming.

"One more question, sir", Eka said.

"Of course, ask", Michael answered.

"This job you are offering my wife, can your wife do it?"

"What sort of question is this? Of course, if my wife needed a job, she would do it. She is an established career woman. She has climbed up the ladder and will not need to be at this level anymore."

"Do I stand any chance, sir?" I inquired.

"Well, I think you've got what it takes but I have never before seen a couple come for an interview for one. Anyway, all the best."

We both walked out and remained silent until we got to the shop. I was downcast. There was no hope for me. I was miserable. I had no money, no job and was at the mercy of a horrid lover. The rest of the day went by. I was low spirited. I did not imagine the dimension of bondage I got myself into. Worse still, I was oblivious of the way out especially in my poor financial state.

Few days later, I contacted one of my friends. We were in the polytechnic as course mates. We shared a level of closeness. Eka knew this. I felt guilty not helping Grace as I ought to, when she relocated to Abuja newly. I neither shared my house nor any other resources with her at her time of need. The tides have somewhat turned. Grace was the only one I could think of as a saving grace.

In and Out

Eka and I have been cohabiting for nearly seven months. One night while I slept, he slipped an engagement ring on my finger. I woke up and saw it. I had very strange feelings about this. I pretended to be happy. "This is so beautiful", I said as I admired the ring. "I'm glad you like it. I hope it keeps your mind at rest about my intentions with you. I love you and I wish for us to be together forever", he responded. Looking at the ring and his behaviour left me utterly confused.

"Grace, please can I move in with you? I don't want to be living with Eka any longer. Being with him is draining." I sent this message to Grace. She was my only option. My other friend, Obia, was squatting with a friend of hers too. *"No problem, let me know when you want to come. I hope you don't have lots of luggage"*, Grace replied. *"Tomorrow. I will come over tomorrow, thank you so much."* My joy knew no bounds. I was getting my freedom in less than 24 hours. I broke this news to Eka.

"I'll be leaving in the morning."

"To?"

"I'm moving in with Grace."

"Grace? Which Grace?"

"The one you know. My friend."

"You said her house was in the slum and not big."

"I have never been to her house. Does it matter anyway? At least I will have my respect and peace of mind."

"You are going nowhere!"

"I will certainly go."

"We shall see!"

I began to pack my things in anticipation.

"I'm sorry Di, I cannot accommodate you. I don't want any trouble. Please stay with your husband and don't call me." Grace sent this message in the middle of the night but I saw it by dawn. I was shattered again. What could have gone wrong? Eka wasn't home when this happened. I cried profusely. My only hope of freedom had just been dashed to pieces. I was frustrated. I had no family in Abuja, Culeta didn't live in Abuja, she was in a neighbouring state. Nyere was living with Culeta at the time. I had only Obia and Grace as friends. The three of us were course mates at school and have been friends since then.

That evening when Eka retuned, I relayed the day's disappointment to him. He was subtly happy. I resigned myself to fate, joined him in his business and we eventually got married. It was not until ten years later, that Grace replayed how Eka used emotional blackmail to make her back down on her offer. Eka was probably obsessed but definitely not in love. I was oblivious of my worth. I gave up my dreams and abilities too soon. I signed off my life to a man on empty promises of love.

In and Out

10

A FARTHER DAY

I, and a few other leaders had the responsibility of making sure the church was set for service, physically and otherwise. It was a small church by every standard; the space, membership, number of years of existence et al. It was a happy church with a feel of home. Eka and I joined the church on the third Sunday of its existence, there were very few of us. I could literally tell the history of the church off the top of my head. I knew when other members joined, the first couple to be wedded, and the first child dedicated in the church; the first programme, and the rest. I was proud to call this church home.

I recall how we made it our home church.

Eka came home after work one day and announced that Pastor had started his church and was inviting us. He had promised to attend. A few days later, I also saw Pastor Bayo in our shop, he invited me too. I assured him that Eka and I had already decided to visit. He was glad. Pastor Bayo used to work in an office two doors away from Eka's previous shop. He resigned from there and founded a consulting firm.

The following Sunday, we were in the church as promised. We looked like a perfect family - husband, wife, two cute toddlers. We had a great time. The next Sunday, Eka suggested we repeat the visit. I reminded him that we had our family church and didn't know why we should be worshipping with God's Peoples Mission. "They are just beginning honey bunch, let us encourage them", Eka replied. For me, as long as it was a Pentecostal church, I did not mind. From attending to help encourage the numbers, we soon attended every Sunday and eventually became permanent members.

I was a front-liner, a role model. I served fervently. It was Father's Day, 2013! Once I set things rolling, I took the back seat

In and Out

except there were other specific functions for the day. As was the norm, on Father's Day, the men took charge of all activities. They were the ushers and the praise team. They acted and sang. They preached and collected offering. It was their day, they held sway. They also dressed copiously. Many brandished their new attire from head to toe. Some changed their walk styles. This was one day a bachelor salivated about being a husband and a dad. It was a colourful day like the others before it. Wives and children also glowed. Some ladies dotted on their men specially. The children were not left out. They knew it was Father's Day Some of them wrote poems and got cards for their dads. Women were happy to help decorate the church hall. Everyone had nothing but good things to say about their husbands. I was conspicuously quiet on this day. My usual self would have led the group of 'virtuous' women who coated the reality they faced in their marriages.

I found out that a lot of seemingly perfect Christian marriages were anything but. The men beat the women, raped and abused them indiscriminately and unremittingly. The church would simply admonish the women to pray harder and endure. Unfortunately for me, my endurance was making me become a bitter woman. I was contemptuous with everyone around me. I had put up a façade for a long time. A few interactions with some of the sisters in church revealed I was not alone. "Why then is everyone living this falsehood?" I wondered.

I tried not to let my mood spoil the day's celebration. Dads are great no doubt but can a bad husband make a great dad? I doubted that. If is he unable to love his wife, how can he love the children without loving their mum? I was in deep reflection. Thankfully, the church provided an enabling environment for such introspection.

In the course of the day's events, the dads pulled their surprises. They had each planned to give their wives a love gift. The women were oblivious of this plot. Once it was time, the Mc charged

In and Out

the men to get their wives to the podium and do what was necessary. The church already knew the 'performing' husbands. There was no way I would not be one of the women. Besides being a paragon, my man was also a showstopper. He was a party life anytime. I loved and hated it simultaneously. Eka took me to the stage. My heart skipped. It paused. It flashed back.

Eka complained of low sales. He had not been paid for his various deliveries. For a few months, we were seriously managing funds while keeping hope alive. I refrained from making demands. I simply asked for the minimum. Once he was short of cash, there was peace and we both enjoyed our positions as husband and wife. This very Father's Day, he did not have money for new clothes but I trusted my man, he's got swag, money or not. He dressed up and carried himself with pomp and pageantry to the church.

We were not talking, keeping malice of some sort. One of our typical misunderstandings had happened the day before and as usual, it lingered. To think that a church girl like me kept malice! It was unbelievable. Thank God the contents of the heart were not open to human scrutiny.

As expected, he was one of the husbands called to the stage to surprise their wives. He led me to the stage in a most romantic way, another charade! Else, how does one correlate the fact that this was a woman whose greetings he didn't acknowledge when he woke up? None could have fathomed the depth of hurt I nursed from the night before. I watched as other men gave their ladies love gifts. I was jittery. "This man was broke", I thought. "Why did he agree to participate in this? What would he give me?" I was not sure what to expect when it got to my turn.

"Honeybunch (that was what he called me), you know I love you?"
"Yes, I do."

In and Out

We both were good with putting up unplanned acts. One reason I was always completely broken by his incessant pranks and cheats was that he knew I could match his game but for my church heart.

"Here is what I have for you." He handed me a cheque. I opened it. It had one hundred thousand naira written in my favour. I screamed and shouted and hugged him and kissed him, all on the church stage. There was a thunderous ovation! We have always been a couple others emulated. We did not disappoint. The hugging, the kissing and the display of love was incredible. Only the devil would have been convinced that this was an act. Ours beat the rest of the couples. We stole the day.

It was the biggest drama we ever put up. A lie can happen on a church stage too. The euphoria remained until service was over. We went home in separate cars just like we came.

In the cool of the day, I was reminiscing. I judged it the mother of all acts. "How did I find the boldness to deceive the entire church?" I searched my heart. I hoped that this was a true reconciliation, perhaps we will make up in bed.

"You know there is no money in that account, right?" Eka interrupted my thoughts.
"I thought as much. I was about asking when you got money."
"Give me back the cheque. I just had to do that to save my face in church."
"Really?" I shook my head.
"Once I get money, I will give it to you, don't worry."

"Give me? Have you ever given me such an amount?"

"What is a hundred thousand? Just give me the cheque, I will surprise you."

"Indeed! How about I keep the cheque and once there is money, you let me know?"

In and Out

"Just give it to me, let's not argue over this, please. We've had a good day. At least, everyone applauded us."

"You've always liked to show-off. Take", I handed him the cheque.

I knew my man. The only truth he told was his name but I gave him the benefit of the doubt. I didn't want to be the obstacle in case he planned any nocturnal action later. He targeted the night time for beating hence I termed it 'nocturnal action'. Eka took the cheque, thanked me wryly. He tore it. I understood his action. The money was gone. We were back to statuesque or even worse.

"It was not a Father's Day for me", I said to myself as I lay on my side of the bed. "This is another 'farther' day", then I slept.

11

OPENING THE BOX

When a living thing is boxed, a quake is inevitable. The box is static in size while the thing inside grows.

I seemed to have arrived at the peak of not just my troubled marital journey, but my dissatisfaction with life. Happiness had eluded me. I remained slim, not out of desire, but frustration. My daily schedule was dangerously boring. The children were dropped off at school; I got back home to clean, tidy and cook. We did not live in a mansion. It was just a three-bedroom flat. I could finish the cleaning in the twinkling of an eye. Besides house chores and family duties, I yearned for financial independence. I knew it would give me respite but much more than that, I wanted relevance. I wanted to add value to my world. Being a wife and a mother was not enough. I wanted more from life. I felt like a prisoner. I was in a box. I was no different from a crumpled piece of paper. These feelings were beginning to weigh me down. Life was much more than I was already experiencing. I felt so. I wanted to live life instead of merely existing. Life is good.

From home, I made efforts to continue contributing to the shop activities. I followed up on contract supplies and payments but was no longer reporting daily at the shop. I made suggestions and checked the records intermittently. I had already set up a structure. I wanted the shop to run systematically. We both did not need to be physically present for the shop to thrive. I did not want to own a business that depended on my physical presence to survive. I did not have the mentality of a petty trader from Nnewi. We disagreed on this. I quit. I opted to stay home. I looked after the children and started thinking out

85

what to do with my life. After all, with all the efforts I made, I did not have any spending right. Eka and I could not even share the same vision. We fought over everything. We disagreed on all matters. Sometimes, I wondered how we agreed to get married. The injunction by the holy book that two cannot work together except there is agreement was very true in our lives. We never agreed. He reminded me that the shop was in existence before I came into his life. The shop was his vision and I had no right to make it mine. I gave up. I stopped working full time in the shop and started minding the home. It was solely my decision. I figured it would give us space and save the constant bickering that was beginning to happen at work. "Why should I bother working full time when there is no direct monetary compensation? As his wife and mother of his children, he would have taken care of his family if I was not working, wouldn't he?" I convinced myself as I stayed back. Eka was not happy about it. He did not understand what my problem was. To him, he offered me a good life, a life of being under his wings. Sometimes, I wondered if he understood the effects of his acts on another life. Perhaps animals could survive but no human being can be gagged for too long. It was choking to say the least. I was fighting for my life as I felt life being snuffed out of me.

I enrolled in a French school close to home. I was clearly destabilized. How to deal with a man like Eka was a nightmare. Anything that gave me temporal happiness was a great idea. The French school did. It was a relief, a breath of fresh air. Attendance was thrice a week. I met new friends who were mostly ladies. I did not have to discuss my challenges with anyone. I simply learnt from their stories, and my resolve to get the best of life became stronger. Everyone was learning the language to help improve their job

86

opportunities. I was the only one in the class who had no agenda. I was learning it for fun. It was indeed fun for nine months.

I thought about selling children's learning resources. I made a proposal to Eka, he bought the idea. He supported me. I travelled to England and bought some items for resell. I was looking happy again. I sold from the trunk of my car. Unfortunately, this business did not succeed. I was desperately trying to find my purpose and my passion. I tried selling a few other things – children's clothes, diapers and fabrics. I concluded that buying and selling was not my calling. Perhaps I should not have married at the time I did. I should have found my purpose first.

Eka taunted me for failing. He called me a lazy, good-for-nothing woman. I knew myself more than anyone in the world. I refused to see the glass half empty. I would not give up on trying to find my happiness and become financially independent. I kept being a wife and a full-time mum. I decided to volunteer more time for church activities. I took on lots of tasks and ran errands. I was happy to be occupied. Soon, I started thinking I had a pastoral calling. I saw myself acting in that capacity, dreaming of attending a bible college and ministering salvation and healing to those in need. I would use my spare time to visit church members, make follow up calls and send text messages. Around 6:00am every day, after my routine morning meditation, I sent a Bible verse to all the church members using an internet short messaging service platform. Soon, the whole church looked forward to receiving my morning dose as I called it. I knew all members' birthdays and marriage anniversaries. I would remind the whole church and urge everyone to send out love to them. The church never had it this good. Someone volunteered quality service at no cost. I was timely for every programme and was usually one of the last to leave the church premises. Indeed, my love for God was admirable.

In and Out

In all of these, there was a dissatisfaction lurking inside me. As the church prepared to celebrate her sixth anniversary, a man of God was invited from Lagos. I was to make reservations for his stay. I drove to the Hilton Hotel. I concluded the necessary reservation and was heading back home. I noticed a black jeep trailing me. I took the first turn, the driver, who was male, also turned, I made another turn at the next junction and he followed this time signaling with his traffic light. I pulled over to know what the matter was. A rich looking, well-dressed man, probably in his fifties came to my window.

"I have been chasing you and you kept running, what is wrong with you?"

"I'm so sorry sir, I didn't know. Good afternoon, sir."

"How are you?"

"Fine, sir", I answered worried at who he was and what he wanted.

"What of your husband?"

"He is fine, sir." I made my way out of the car at the mention of husband. In my mind, the man must know me well enough to ask about Eka.

"My name is Solarin Soye."

"I am Mrs Chima. Odinaka Chima, sir."

"Here is my card, can I have yours?"

At this point, I became unsure of his motive, if he knew Eka or me. My patience and courtesy were simply because I believed he was an insider. Usually, I do not give room for male admiration. I thought that once a chance was given, men latched on it and wrecked a good girl's home. My naivety was out of this world. Besides being a Christian woman, I had to be a role model for my members. I was never to be caught with another man, seriously or jokingly.

"I don't have a card, sir."

"Where do you work?"

"I don't work, sir."

"Your husband must be a very rich man."

"Why do you say so sir?"

"A woman like you with a big car and looking good, your husband must be rich to maintain your lavish lifestyle when you don't work."

"It's not really correct, sir."

"You mean you can work if you see an opportunity?"

"Of course, I will definitely work. Can you help me get a job?"

"What kind of job would you love to do?"

"Any job, sir. Administrative work, any job, sir."

"You seem a patient person, why not open a school?"

"Patient? How? I'm not sure I am."

"It would take a patient person to be standing with me for almost ten minutes, talking with a person she doesn't know."

"Well, I am only being respectful, that's what I owe you at least."

"You should work with children, open a school."

In and Out

"I don't know much regarding that but if I have the money, I sure will. How about you open one and I run it for you?"

"I already have a school."

"Employ me, please."

"I can call for them to interview you, if you scale through, you will be employed. I will not interfere in the process, okay?"

"Alright, sir. Thank you very much."

"Call me, you have my card."

"I certainly will. Thank you very much, sir."

We parted. This must be an angel, I thought. I pinched myself to be sure it was not a dream.

The next day was a Saturday, I called Mr Solarin who confirmed my interview for Monday, 10:00am. What joy I had! For nothing but a twist of fate, my phone spoilt the next day, Sunday. All my efforts to rectify it were abortive. The only option was to give it to Eka to help take it for repairs as the commander in chief and minister of finance of our home.

Eka was the sole custodian of the family purse. He determined how high or low everyone went. He approved the exact time, place and the type of life any of his subordinates should have. He flaunted his lordship unapologetically. To him, he was a king and his subjects were his two children, his wife and anyone who took shelter in his palace temporarily or permanently. He made the money, he called the shots. He wielded the power. He sought no advice from his main subject – his wife.

In and Out

When Eka returned home from work, I was full of hope that he fixed my phone and I looked forward to getting it back from him. It was my simplicity that made me give him the phone anyway. If it were him, he would never have done so. For ninety-five percent of the years we were married, I dared not touch his phone. When he buys a new phone, I could just see it from a distance but not touch it. I remember the day he nearly broke my hand because I refused to drop his phone. He was sleeping or so I thought, I took the phone to admire it, it was a new phone. He roared and asked me to drop it. I ran into the toilet and locked the door. He used his leg and kicked the door open. He gave me a slap, twisted my arms until I dropped it. Eka was mean like that. I recall with sadness the day we almost had an accident. He was driving and asked me to buy airtime. I bought it from the nearest vendor and made for his phone to help him. He started struggling with me with one hand and the other on the steering. I was utterly shocked. We struggled until he gave up. I was prepared to have an accident instead of giving him back the phone. He gave up. I recharged his airtime and as well checked his messages and saw his atrocities with his lovers. He probably was embarrassed but did not show it. He never apologised. All his three phones were securely passworded. As life improved for us, he got a Macintosh for himself; he also secured it with a password known to him alone.

I could not fathom how a man with skeletons in his shelf had the effrontery to question me. My simplicity was foolery!

He walked straight to the room where I was and began his interrogation.

"Who is Mr Solarin?"

"He is a man helping me get a job in a school."

91

In and Out

"How come I don't know about him? When and where did you meet him?"

"He called? What did he say?"

"How dare you ask me? Tell me everything about him!"

"Please, can I have my phone if it is fixed?"

"He said your interview is confirmed for Tuesday, 10:00am. What interview is that?"

"I just told you he is helping me get a job in a school."

"So, who is he? Where did you meet him? For how long have you guys been on?"

"I met him on Friday; he wants to help me get a job in a school he co-owns. That's all."

"Don't even bother; you will not work in any school. Did I not tell you I don't want a working wife? Anyway, let's see who is in charge. Call him back and tell him to cancel the interview and not to call you ever again! And let me warn you, I am your husband. I must know everything that goes on in your life. You must inform me. You have no choice, I am your husband. I am in charge of this house and everything inside!"

There was silence.

I got my phone back. I refused to be shaken. I had heard his ramblings many times. I was used to his noise even though I get rattled when he reiterates them. The effects were ephemeral. I made the necessary follow up. My mind was made up. I was going for the

In and Out

interview. I would work and nothing was going to stop me. This was seven years after marriage. Freedom is not inside a box.

I contacted Mr Solarin and got clarity on the interview. It was scheduled for 10:00am on Tuesday. I waited and attended albeit anxiously. I had a written test the first day followed by a meeting with a panel of interviewers. When it looked uncertain about my position, I offered to work for a full month without pay and if I worked well, I could be retained for a salary. This option blew the minds of the panel. I was offered a job. I was to resume the first Monday in September, the start of the new session.

As happy as I was, I knew there was one more bridge to cross. I told my pastor who was at the time the only one I looked up to. Pastor Bayo knew my situation. He had often intervened in our marriage. He prayed, counselled and encouraged. Once when Eka got a contract and could not execute it, Pastor Bayo lent him two million Naira cash and also introduced him to a seller where Eka got a huge credit facility at no cost. He wished our family well as any revered man of God should. He was however often disappointed at Eka's position on certain matters.

"You will have to embark on a seven-day fast."

"Seven days? Oh my God!"
"What else can you do? Prayer remains the only way. God will touch his heart; he will allow you to work."

"When is the start?"

"Tomorrow."

A humble admonition of live and let live was a very complex sentence for Ekachukwu Chima. How else would he exert his authority

In and Out

as the head of the home? I wondered if the slave rule of centuries imprinted this servant-master relationship on his mind. It was not uncommon to see the unpretentious reason of having absolute control over a woman. The ladies were also brought up to see their position as wives as a privileged one that must be guarded jealously. The church preached it, the society enforced it.

I religiously fasted. God was all I knew. Right from my early teenage years, I opted for God. I did my best to maintain my stance. I derailed a bit here and there but always hoped in God as my only helper. I fasted and prayed privately. I trusted God wholly and was very optimistic about being allowed to work. At the end of the fasting period, I met with Pastor Bayo in his office. We both had a fervent prayer session. Pastor Bayo prayed like a machine, he could go on for hours. After the session, he promised to talk to Eka and encouraged me to keep hope in God. The prayers worked. Eka allowed me to resume work.

I knew he reluctantly gave his consent but I didn't care. I was very satisfied that at least I was going to be useful to an organization, and earn money for myself too. It was a renowned private primary school for the cream of the crop. The children were from the upper middle and top classes. Certainly, I knew that I was in a privileged position. I worked with the primary section. I coordinated administrative activities. While working, my passion for teaching began to bud. I worked very hard. I won the owner's heart in a short while. Eka was always disgruntled about this, especially knowing that another man was instrumental to his wife's happiness.

For me, this was victory. I had won a battle.

In and Out

12

THE PRISONER OF FREEDOM

I had a tail. I was followed everywhere. My only offence was my insistence on working and earning money. Eka sniffed his way into the school. He had to show off his superiority over his wife. "If you try me, I will come to that your office and mess you up", he often threatened. "Tell them your husband says so", was another constant line. He sounded like he owned the Federal Republic of Nigeria.

Eka was an insecure man. His insecurity when encountered, always left a bitter taste; it had everyone absolutely shocked. The signs that I overlooked before marriage reared their heads, this time excessively. I wished I hadn't gone ahead with the union. Living in agony and regret every day, I voiced my frustration to him. "I regret marrying you", I would say. "I don't want this marriage anymore", I would whine whenever I felt low. I was going nuts. "This marriage only brings out the worst in me. I barely recognise my sweet self", I thought.

I had always seen myself as a very simple lady. I was moderate in all ramifications. My dressing, make-up, food, desires, everything. None could use the word - ostentation, with me. I could give up anything on earth. I was just a girl next door. I did not flaunt anything. I did not think there was any need. Occasionally, I heard people talk about me as being beautiful and intelligent. Many people expressed their surprise when they know that I was a housewife. "How could you possibly be home doing nothing? Are you not wasting your life?" they would ask. "My Oga does not want a working wife" I would respond. In order to preserve the sanctity of marriage as I was taught, I shielded

95

my husband from all forms of abuse. I spoke highly of him, submitted my will and everything else without a fight. I gave up my life, my career, my taste and my desires. I dressed the way Eka wanted. I had no style, no friends, and no future. I knew these. They were not what I wanted for myself but family above all was my mantra. I was willing to give up my life. I did.

My function at school was not as easy as I envisaged. My closing time was 5:00pm and I rarely closed at that time. I worked so hard, sometimes I went to work on Saturdays. Besides trying to be the best at my job, I needed to show loyalty to my boss. The usual school breaks were not part of my entitlement. I worked part of the holidays, a lot of private school staff did. The administrative department however, never completely closed because of the quest for students. I used my break times to pick up the children from their school to the house and back to work. They were not used to a working mum and soon began to complain. They were dropped early and picked late. It was a bit difficult for them to adjust to my new schedule. The demands of working took its toll on me. As with many other white-collar jobs, there were downtimes, bickering and unnecessary bureaucracy. There were so many areas my expectations were not met. I found out that Mr Solarin was neither an owner nor a co-owner. He was simply a very good parent who protected the school owner from the wimps and caprices of discontented parents. Eka called Mr Solarin a few times to express his displeasure with my closing time. He saved his number the day he helped me fix my phone. Mr Solarin, a gentleman, always encouraged him and never informed me of my husband's paroxysms.

Eka found a reason to lambast my decision to work. I tried to rebuff him. I pushed back as much as I could. The result was absence of peace in our haven. This man had too strong a hold on me. The ease with which I quit everything else to fulfill his wish was inexplicable.

96

On the one hand, I wanted my freedom, on the other, I gave it up too soon to make him happy. Again, I made the ultimate sacrifice, I quit the job. Seeming peace returned. I was always alone in my decisions. I never took recourse to my immediate family. Eka did not want a close relationship with my family. I was foolish to adhere. Besides Nyere who visited me seldomly and Juni, my youngest sister who lived with me at a time, no one else in my family knew how Eka and I lived. Those two could tell that Eka was only a good man by looks. If he had his way, he would have banned them from visiting. He tried to exert his control over them but met resistance. My siblings knew better than to run anyone's home down. Generally, we respected each other's boundaries. They did the same with Culeta and Obi. Eka was overly highhanded. He talked like the world was at his feet. He disregarded all his in-laws. He thought himself a rich man. He was imperious.

Eka felt working opened my eyes a bit. He further reiterated his unsaid house rule – you are not allowed to go out alone. If you must go out, go with the kids or with me. What a queer rule I thought. "What sort of stupid rule is that?" I queried. I was not known for many words. I kept my cool. I had become used to living a caged life. Apart from church functions, I hardly attended any other social events. My friends were in church. My events were church events. Despite the fact that Eka knew all the church members, a church with less than a hundred members, he was still unsatisfied having his wife with them. For him, his wife belonged to him alone and should serve his children and him for as long as she lived.

I practically spent all my spare time in church. On Sundays, I left about 6:30am and returned no earlier than 4:00pm. This was long before my short stint as a church staff. On Saturdays, I was in church from noon till night. On Thursdays, I was there from 4:00pm till 9:00pm. On other days, I either worked for the church from home or

In and Out

visited brethren. Each time I was in church, I went with the children. I enjoyed being with them. I was the chief correspondence officer. I kept the data of all church members and kept tabs on all, a job I gave myself. No wonder the opportunity to be an administrative assistant was naturally bequeathed to me. My presence commanded a lot of respect. It was possible Eka was intimidated. He saw how much I was regarded. When I spoke, I did so with a certain command. My voice and sentences were graceful. Me, a woman that won the hearts of most church members was coerced and boxed by one man.

"Who was the man that you were talking to, two days ago?"

"I don't get you."

"You came out of your car and you were talking to a man, who was he?""

"I don't understand you, what man? When? Where?"

"Did you not talk to any man? His car was very close to yours, I think he brushed your car or so?"

"Oh! He did, I came out to see if there was any impact but there was none. I let him go."

"But you guys spoke for a while."

"Of course, we did."

"What were you talking about and why didn't you tell me about it?"

"Chicf police officer, find out the remaining details from your reporters."

This was one of the standoffs between my investigator husband and myself. My worry was what he was turning the children into. He

In and Out

found time to always ask the children how the day went, where we went and what we did. I would not know his intentions for doing so. I was simply uncomfortable with the effects of such tasks on the youngsters. I remembered my days with Asumpta and how he turned her to my personal bodyguard.

Every night, Eka checked through my phone. When I changed my password, he sent the children to find out the new one from me. When Eka checked my messages, he sometimes replied, deleted his response, leaving no traces. Some others, he sent to his mail and further printed out. It was not as if he found any evidence of infidelity in all his searching. One was left to wonder his motive. If a husband intended to build his partner, would he be looking for what was not? I was constantly in a mire of confusion about this man.

I had a childhood friend called Kene. He was very close to my siblings especially my older brother, Obi. We teased, mocked each other and had great laughter. We lost contact as we grew and left our birth city for greener pasture. This was before the arrival of mobile phones. One day, Obi visited me from his Lagos base. He asked to be taken to Kene's office. Apparently, they maintained their contact. Through this visit, I was glad to reconnect with Kene. He was married just like me. As teenagers, we never dated; there was never any emotional involvement. Having reconnected, we chatted not so frequently. We relived our childhood memories and resumed our taunts. For both of us, we had fun. We never met. Our phones were our meeting point. Eka saw our chats. It was difficult to tell if he was angry or jealous. He forwarded the chats to Obi and requested to have Kene stay away from his wife. Obi in turn did as was requested. Kene cut me off. I was oblivious of the chain of event.

99

In and Out

In my mind, I dare say Eka was a sadist. He had his boys outings, came home late, travelled around the globe with his women, lived as he pleased but kept a prisoner. I had a new company called misery. It is paradoxical to come from a middle class with so much anxiety and gloom. My cheerfulness had completely vanished. I became belligerent, always ready to attack. How could any good thing come out of such a soul? How could anyone do such to another human? Worse still, Eka did not notice how emaciated I was becoming. Perhaps he did, but preferred it that way. The more he pulled strings, the more volatile I became and the more he used it against me.

"If this is your idea of vacation, count me out. Consider this the last time I will embark on a trip you orchestrated, I thundered in my loudest voice when I got back from my last trip to the United States with my children. I was the most miserable person on that trip; just like any other trip we had been on. I reminisced on the restricted movement and complete lack of choice. From the visa application to the interview, I was usually a robot. He told me what to say. I nodded and executed without questioning. He prepared all the documents. He wrote the letters. He conjured the bank statement. He made the fake hotel reservations. He did everything. For the British visa that did not need a physical appearance, he submitted all that was necessary and simply had the rest of his subjects go with him for finger print and submission. He was the head of this kingdom - he worked, walked and talked so. On one hand, this could have been great and commendable but one's wife and children were not his subjects. The work a man does to advance his family should be appreciated indeed.

When we got to the United States, we were picked up at the airport by our host, Ify. This was our first meeting. Ify's husband was Eka's friend. Everyone was happy. I had only eight hundred dollars for

In and Out

the four- week planned vacation with two children. How much could that do? This money was for everything – feeding, transportation, sightseeing and shopping. The possibility of this amount being enough would have been magical.

As I stayed with our host family, they fed us and took care of every extra expense we incurred. I thought it wise to make some contributions for the feeding. Four weeks was a long time for someone to feed an adult and two children hence I felt the need to help. As my manner was, I had to ask for permission. If I exhausted the money with me, I had to give a satisfactory account. In retrospect I wonder what would have happened if I hadn't. I wish I hadn't!

"I would like to buy some foodstuff for the house, at least a hundred dollars' worth."

"Buy what? Why? Did they say you should buy foodstuff?"

"Come on, that's the least I can do. The children and I eat from this house. They are not super rich and even if they were, should we not contribute? For goodness sake, you can't dump your family on another."

"Food is cheap in America. Don't spend your money on food. If you choose to do so, it will be to your detriment."

I paid no attention to his tantrum. I made my contribution albeit fifty dollars.

How can a sensible being think like this? I mused as I cried. I was the one on a vacation with two children from Nigeria in America. Every morning, after helping with chores, I had the children shower and eat after which we all turned to the television. How could I come this distance just to watch television? It was barely a week and the

In and Out

three of us were wishing to get back to Nigeria. We could not visit any tourist area for lack of money. By the time I calculated the transportation and entrance fee and entertainment, I stayed back and watched the television. Our host was unsure how much money I had come with, and wanted an easier life for me. She suggested that I hired a car without knowing that hiring a car was the least of my problems. I had just a few dollars to rely on till he came. For all the family vacations we had, we, the subjects went first. The king arrived about ten days to the end of the vacation to change the game. The children looked forward to his coming. To them, their mum was always boring and poor. This was probably one of his objectives for making sure he was solely in charge of the family treasury; he got to buy off their love. One would wonder why he would not empower his wife. He loved flaunting his ego. He wanted everyone to know him as the action man. He desired that he be the centre of attention and the point of reference. He had his way, constantly. The rest of the vacation was uninteresting to say the least. No one should ever go on vacation as a prisoner, I convinced myself. I was not working. I had no money. The man at the helm of affairs controlled the purse to the last dime. I bore this treatment for four consecutive trips. This became my last.

In tears, I recounted my trip to Cambridge for a conference. Eka from the comfort of his bed arranged this trip to the letter. "Make sure that when you get to Heathrow, use the black cabs", he said. "Ask them to take you straight to the hotel." I did. I got into a black cab and was very comfy until the metre began to roll. While on the way to the hotel, he was chatting and monitoring my progress. Ordinarily, this would have been romantic but knowing his motive, I did not consider it so. Not until I caught him with his lady in our home did I understand the full import of the policing. He simply did not want other men to do to his wife what he did with ladies. At the end of the one-week

In and Out

conference at Cambridge, I was to return to the hotel close to Heathrow for easy access to the airport. I did not use the taxi. I opted to go with a friend who knew the cheapest train route, but not before we did some shopping. By the time I got to the hotel, I got the news. "Madam, your husband has been calling, he's terribly worried calling all the way from Nigeria", the receptionist said. "I'm sorry. Tell him I'm here now. He will definitely call back", I responded. I did not bother turning on my phone. I needed some peace of mind else he would have berated my friend and the shopping.

The worst of the manipulations was what I dubbed 'car control'. Eka gave me two thousand naira for fuel each week. According to him, if I was strictly on school runs, the money would suffice for the week. If, however, the fuel ran out before the end of the week, I would have to give a satisfactory account of my movements. I was straight-jacketed; home - drop off – home – pickup – home. Somedays, I went to church. Such days were covered by the fuel money. He loved having me ask for money, he relished being in control of my life. Once in a while, he gave money for the house needs. I had to submit a working list if I hoped to get replenished in the coming months. Not only would he go through the list, he would also find his way to the kitchen and everywhere else checking and verifying! If by his estimate, the money was not used up, I was unlikely to get a dime. It would not matter if the children were starving. How a meagre two thousand naira's worth of petrol was supposed to suffice for a week was unfathomable. Eka once said, "When a woman has money, she begins to misbehave." I wished to know how he lived with Mary. From the facts I gathered, she worked with an international non-profit organization.

"Sister Di, why did you tell your husband you gave me a ride home?"

103

In and Out

"What do you mean?

"He came to harass me. He said that one day my wife will give him a ride too. If I did not want such, I should stay away from you."

"Not again!" I snapped.

This would be the umpteenth time Eka warned the men in our small church to stay away from his wife. They were not allowed to sit near me in church. I was to stay beside ladies only. If for any reason it happened, the man must not make any form of communication, eye contact, body contact, whispering or smiling. Almighty Eka would be watching from behind and would surely approach with his venom.

A prisoner is not always behind bars.

In and Out

THE LAST CHRISTMAS

The day was drawing close. I was sure we were not travelling to the village for Christmas. In my ten years of marriage, I had only visited Eka's village for Christmas once. Eka's grandfather insisted on seeing his grand-children. Eka made it happen. It was memorable.

The twins were six months old that Christmas. A few days after we visited, they were baptised following the Roman Catholic doctrine. Nne was at the fore of the activities. It must have been her idea. She knew the priests. She made all the arrangements. She invited and entertained her guests. Nasa fell sick a few days later. Eka was visibly worried. Nasa was suspected to be allergic. In six months, she had been in and out of the hospital a number of times. We were yet to figure out what she was allergic to. Grandma Ndem, Nne and other women made suggestions of how we should treat the fever and cold. Their suggestions spanned orthodox and herbal medicines. None suggested going to the doctor. The closest general hospital was at Nnewi, a town about forty minutes away. It was nearly midnight. Eka spoke to the paediatrician on the phone. He recommended some analgesics and antimalarial drugs. I came with Panadol syrup so we administered. By morning, grandma Ndem brought some herbal mixture for us to give Nasa. We know better than to do such. There was a misunderstanding. Eka went to find the nearest reliable pharmacy. The East was renowned with the selling of fake drugs. One had to be careful. When he got back, he proposed that we returned to Abuja. There was an outburst from all corners. "Does it mean we can no longer look after a child?" "Why are you leaving because of

105

In and Out

ordinary fever?" "Are there not children who are born here, do they not survive?" "You are belittling us!".

There were so many complaints. I was still. I prayed silently. Nasa recovered. The holiday continued. Grandpa amused us all through. He was a sweet soul, a great company. The next time we would come home was for his burial. I wished the twins knew him more.

Going to the village was never Eka's idea of life. This was unlike a typical man from the eastern part of the country. The end of the year which coincided with Christmas celebration was a time to compare notes. It was usually for stock taking. Young men were proud to return from every nook and cranny. They brought their human and non-human properties for show. Mothers looked forward to seeing their sons display their year's achievement subtly and overtly. Those who had built new houses invited others for house warming ceremonies. There were marriages, chieftaincy title taking and all sorts of celebrations every end of the year. Men who had achieved less were uncomfortable about going home. Their people may not be very proud of them. Achievement varied from marrying a new wife to having children, to buying cars, building houses, graduating from school and so on. Men were encouraged to add a feather to their cap.

By all standards, Mr and Mrs Chima ought to be happy as a couple. They had children within the first two years of being married. Eka's businesses was growing. Lack of finance and absence of children were mostly the two areas that brought about friction in most homes. This was not the case with the Chimas. Could it be that there were some irregularities with the motive of the marriage? Eka had no child with his first wife of three years. There was a break up, he was never comfortable discussing the details with me. I felt he must have

In and Out

been at fault going by my experience. Sometimes, I thought Eka just wanted children, having got them, he cared less about me.

Once I confirmed that we were not traveling for the yuletide, I treated my family to a variety of meals depending on the availability of funds. My mother-in-law got used to us not returning for Christmas like everyone else. She probably held it against me but pretended. I tried to maintain a good relationship with her. Most mothers-in-law from her part of the country and of her age were swayed by material things. Unfortunately, I did not have much. Eka on the other hand, did not alleviate the situation. He would not give me money. This gave the impression that I did not want to help.

Every year, Pastor Bayo declared an end of year fast for the entire church starting from the 26th of December. All members went to church in the evening to pray and break the fast together. This lingered through the coming year with a break on the first day of the year only. I religiously followed the ritual It afforded the entire church a good end of the year and a sober start to the new year. Eka on the other hand, made a choice of when to participate. Our marriage was merely ephemeral. There was nothing deep. One could tell from a short meeting that the relationship had no anchor. A break up was just a matter of time. I knew this regardless of my fears. Eka probably knew it, too.

Depth is vital to any lasting relationship. Beauty, money, deception, manipulation, intimidation and the likes can only go so far, this was my continuous thought.

"How about we check into a hotel on the 24th and return on the 26th? I really don't want to cook and waste the food because there will

In and Out

be no one to eat, and church fasting commences immediately", I suggested to Eka.

"You are so extravagant! Just look at a wife's suggestion! To stay in a hotel for Christmas, where is your decency?" he retorted.

I was flabbergasted. I was hoping for a family get away, a time to bond, and be served upon. I did not mean any harm. I knew there was nothing wrong with my suggestion. I knew my man, he was intimidating me again. I understood what romance was. I was simply with a partner who did not speak my language. I was frustrated. The thickness of the separation wall was increasing. It was not clear how a simple suggestion as this made Eka walk out of the house and not return for a few days.

In the early evening of 24th December, Eka returned home. "Pack your bag, we are leaving for the hotel", he said. I had mixed feelings not knowing what to make of his proposition. This was the same reason he did not sleep in the house for nearly three days. What happened? What changed? While pondering, I packed my bags and got the children ready. Eka drove us down to the hotel and made sure we were properly settled. We ordered dinner and were relaxing. "Let me tidy a few things up, I'll join you guys shortly." Eka excused himself. He came back past midnight. There was no excuse. Abuja is not known for heavy traffic, least of all, during a festive period and also an end of year. I was sleepless waiting for him. I called his phone a few times but he would not take the call. I was apprehensive. Is this getaway a blessing or a curse? I kept pondering until Eka knocked on the door. I opened not particularly with a smile. I was hoping to have his reasons but none came forth. I asked but was ignored. The family was in one big room. By the time the children went to bed, I made for his love. I went close and hoped for body contact. He did not

In and Out

reciprocate. I went back to my shell. "What could have been the reason for agreeing to stay over in a hotel? We could have simply stayed back home." I was as confused as ever. I knew this was all over. My heart told me to stop bothering.

The next morning, we went for breakfast. There was a crowd at the dining area.

"Goodness! So, many families do this?"

"Do what?"

"Spend their holidays in hotels."

"I'm glad you can see."

"Where did you learn this from? Who taught you?"

"Meaning?"

"You have never suggested it."

"I don't understand you, I really don't"

"What don't you understand? You are too full of yourself!"

The conversation at the breakfast table was leading to an argument. I thought that a reasonable man would have been grateful and made the best of this situation. It was supposed to be family time. Unfortunately, Eka reasoned from the other side of his brain. The table was not fun after all. We soon finished and went back to our room. Before lunch, the children went to the pool. I was happy to have brought their swimming trunks. Eka made an uncomplimentary remark about this. He thought that since I had put things together so well, I would have been influenced by another person. Definitely, he did not have the courtesy of ascribing some intelligence to his wife. What was

In and Out

the essence of marrying a woman and vilifying her? Hatred was definitely fully brewed. The relationship was sticky and sickly.

"Later in the evening, you guys should go and visit Lilian and her family" ordered my lord and master.

'We?' I enquired. You are not going with us?

"I will drop you guys off. She can bring you back or use a taxi."

"If we are not all going, then let's forget it."

"You like trouble. You make a mountain out of a molehill. Must I go with you? Can't you let the children play with her children? You are an enemy of progress", he persisted.

Lilian, according to him, was a member of staff of the Government parastatal where Dr. Shehu worked and from whom he got some contracts. They, Lilian and Eka had become very close. The degree of their closeness was known to only both of them. I smelt a rat but kept it to myself. Lilian was married to an elderly man who also worked in a Government parastatal. Lilian and her husband were reasonably well off. She tried to get close to me but I was skeptical of her motive. It was not uncommon to see ladies who are lovers to a man get very close to his wife. It is regarded as operating within a safe zone. The lady lover knows the pulse of both her victims. My instincts would not allow her into my personal space. For peace's sake, we visited Lilian and her family just as Eka would have it. That was how the Christmas day was spent. The next day, we returned home. Fasting started in church.

The New Year rolled in; I was engrossed in the fast. My prayer this time was different. On the 7th of January, I wrote Eka an email …

In and Out

My Dear Husband,

This morning, I asked you if you said something to Pastor about us or me. You answered that you didn't say anything to him. I knew you comprised the truth like you always do. I have always doubted you because you have given me a thousand reasons to. I am copying him on this mail because it seems to me that you like middle men in our marriage.

I would have preferred that Jesus be the third party in our affairs but no, you usually will not get Him involved, you prefer human beings.

I have ceased to pray for the success of our marriage. I know that soon I will also stop making efforts for it to work. I take full responsibility for my decision to be your wife. I completely regret my decision. Today, albeit very painful, I accept that I should not have been involved with you at all. Looking at how we started, and how we have continued to this day, I am afraid of how we will continue. It is only faith in God that has kept me this far.

Consider the following:

1.   We cannot have a decent conversation, we don't communicate.
2.   We have NEVER shared our dreams and aspirations. Therefore, we don't have a common cause that we are pursuing as a family.
3.   10years gone and we are still cumbered with such frivolous matters as hiring a house help.
4.   We do not trust each other. I particularly do not trust you.
5.   We don't make love – you just want a woman to go into and come out whenever you want! I am a woman!!!!
6.   We are not transparent with each other; I barely know who you are!
7.   We don't even pray together, we don't share the same faith – I honestly do not know where you stand as far as God and relationship with Him is concerned.
8.   We don't have common perspectives as far as raising children and having a family.

9. We are not friends, we CANNOT work together, we do not sleep together, what do we even share?

Why then are we married? This is a question I have asked myself many times and I cannot find an answer.

I should not have made this costly mistake! I thought I could live with it but surely, I can no longer do so. I prayed today and I will keep praying for this marriage to end. Hopefully, may it end peacefully. I am particularly tired of the embarrassments it causes me.
May I use this opportunity to tell you that I hold nothing against you. I take full responsibility for accepting to be your wife. I didn't weigh the consequences of my actions before I ventured. I didn't seek advice from ANYONE. I didn't consider the signs that I saw. Today, I am paying for my mistake. I am consoled that today is another morning. As far as I have life, I can always start over again.

111

In and Out

Eka showed everyone my email. He was proud to show it off. It was the license he longed for. He printed it and flaunted it. "My wife has ended our marriage", he shouted from the roof top.

A fool is a fool. Thinking about his act, I recalled a favourite maxim of my mathematics teacher in secondary school; *he who knows not and does not know that he knows not is a compound, complex, complicated, confused fool*. I would not know who was a fool, Eka or I. I think I was.

Eka did not see that this letter was pregnant with his failures. He did not have the capacity to accomplish a basic life skill of communication. To him, I did not want to be a wife. I did not want to submit. I did not want to be controlled. I was everything but good. I was a frustrated woman who had come to her wit's end. I had peace as soon as I came to terms with the ineptness of my relationship with the man I called husband for years. I completed the fast by the 15th day with the entire church. I focused on my children, stayed on at my new job and remained resolute.

I thought deeply about Eka and his immediate family and my ten years sojourn. His mum was unpredictable. The morning following my traditional marriage rites, I was with Eka's mum. We were getting to know each other. Nne said to me; "A man can marry five wives, he can keep marrying until he finds the right one." I could not forget this sentence. For me, it was the most unwelcoming statement for a new bride. The traditional marriage occurred in the village. By the time we returned to the city, Eka was unwilling to proceed with the statutory

112

In and Out

marriage as we had agreed. I begged Nne to persuade Eka. She was always unwilling. She was rather about me getting pregnant. "Don't worry, concentrate on getting pregnant first. He will do it in God's time." Eka's father never liked me, we never really talked. Eka was the first child. I was close to Nuel, his younger brother. Unfortunately, Nuel was not regarded in the family. He was not rich. He did not seem to have found his path in life. Hence, he had no voice. The typical Igbo man would scorn the wisdom of the poor. Eka seemed to be the all-powerful in his immediate family; he was the heir apparent and the richest at the time.

His mum, the only one that could prevail with her husband and son, was definitely playing pranks with me. Talking to her never yielded any result. My greatest difficulty was where to go from where I was and how the movement would be. The way we would finally end was a mirage. I kept letting the days roll by.

In and Out

14

STAYING AFLOAT

I was lucky to have my friend, Blessing, give a job contact. I went for the interview and scaled through. I was offered a job effective September. This was in July. I was still in our breaking home. Eka was no longer coming home. Most of his daily used personal belongings were no longer in the house. Accepting the end was tough for me. In my innermost being, I wished things had worked out better.

In a bid to stay happy, I quit my job as an administrator in the school and took up employment as a church administrative assistant. This lasted for two months only - April and May. Eka spread the rumour that I was dating Pastor Bayo, a rumour without an iota of truth. Anyone who knew Eka, associated him with lies. He relished the exaggeration and misrepresentation of facts. He was a bully by every standard. He got away with his acts most often, perhaps he selected his targets carefully. At the height of the rumour, Pastor Bayo asked me to quit my church job and pay attention to my home. That may have been the Christian thing to do. I also stepped down from every leadership position I held in church. I stopped appearing at church events. I was dwindling, my light, my smiles, and my glow. The church was praying. By the end of the month of June, I was obviously shrunken. I was the shadow of my ever-bubbling self. I was managing to keep my head above water. While coming to terms with my dying marriage, I had to deal with the rumour of Pastor Bayo and me as ignited by Eka.

Anyone who knew Pastor Bayo would not even mention such a thing near him. He lived a very transparent life. His church office was right next to his wife's office. The demarcation had a conspicuous part

114

In and Out

separated by glass such that one could see the activities in his office. He was the simplest of men. Besides being a Pastor, he was a successful man in all ramifications. His personal business blossomed. He never took a salary from the church. He never cajoled members to donate gifts to him. For him, Pastors should work and not depend on the church for livelihood. Eka had known him for a long time. He knew when Pastor Bayo was an employee and when he became a CEO. He had enjoyed some business loan from him more than once. Even though Eka defaulted with paying back, he still never held it against him.

Eka made a deliberate choice to tarnish his image. He forgot when he was begging for his financial help. It is said that wickedness dwells in the heart of men; nothing could be truer about Eka. This was the man in the early days of our marriage, he ran to for counsel. He told lies about me to him. He made him keep intervening in our affairs. Pastor Bayo could have got tired at some point but he did not show it. He persevered as was his manner. He believed the best out of worst situations.

One Sunday morning, during the regular church prayer meeting, I asked to be prayed for because I was about to take the toughest decision of my life. Everyone was interested in the details but I kept it to my chest. Our society was yet to embrace quitting a marriage as a valid option for Christians. Wives were to keep enduring while fasting and praying. I began to look for help outside my Christian circle. I met a lawyer who became my friend, Barrister Steve. Steve encouraged me to get a job and rebuild my life with my children. He provided insight and checks to what Barrister Martins did. I tried to keep it together. A close discussion with me however, gave me away. I broke down at any slightest reminder of my relationship with the father of my children. I considered myself ruthless, careless, incautious and

In and Out

uncircumspect with my life. I should not have committed even a day of my life to a man like Eka. There was no basis for doing so. We had nothing in common. I took responsibility for the failure of our marriage.

In my quagmire, after the grand fight, unsure of what to do, I got a call from Obi, my brother. "Hello sis''. You know Eka is no longer interested in this marriage, right? While he was in Dubai, I kept encouraging him to go and rebuild his family but he was insistent. I suggest you take care of yourself. You can bring the children to me and sort yourself." Obi said. "Are you aware he is building a house? It seems he had a blueprint he set in motion long before now. I am surprised you did not pick up the signs" he continued. "My house is free, I am your dad even though I am your brother, bring the children to me, take some time off and clear your confusion, then you can come for them. It may not be easy but you surely will overcome" he encouraged further.

"What a sigh of relief, brother. The children have been my greatest worry. For this offer, we are coming tomorrow. I will look for money, we will see you tomorrow." I agreed with him as I hung the phone.

This was a great relief! I would not have stayed this long in the relationship if not for the children. I had always worried where to keep them until I was stable. The offer from Obi was the biggest and best. I put a call to Nyere, a sister of all sisters. My eldest sister Culeta and her husband were deacons in the church. They completely dissociated themselves from my decision to quit. "We are Christians, we do not support divorce", Culeta's husband emphasized. I cared less. With Nyere, Obi and our mum on my side, victory was certain.

In and Out

Obi was my last supporter. He was friendly with Eka. They were age mates and had shared the struggles of growing men, and fathers of young children. They were more like allies than *ogo*. (in-laws). In our early days of marriage, within the first year, Eka voluntarily offered to support Obi's business with one million naira. Obi was grateful for the loan and so were all of us. He promised to pay back in installments. When I put to bed, Obi sent his wife from Lagos to spend a few days with us. On the twins first birthday, we had a big party. Obi sent his wife and two children to help us for a few days. He was my big brother and in the absence of my dad, my father. Yet he stooped for us. He was the one checking on us. Neither the children nor Eka and I had ever spent a night in his house in Lagos all through our ten years together. Whenever Eka had business in Lagos, he slept in a hotel. When Obi had to be in Abuja, he spent the night in our house. There was no air around him. He regarded Eka as a part of our family in word and in deed. I could not report Eka to him seeing their relationship. I bore whatever problems we had. He was disappointed that his intervention yielded no positive outcome. It was not entirely his fault, by the time he intervened, we were irretrievably degenerated. Eka had regard for no one from my family, or any of his friends that I knew.

Before dawn the next morning, I took the children with 3 pairs of clothes each to the car park. The journey out of the union thus began. The date was Thursday, 21st August. While on the trip, I explained to the children what was happening. They had seen the fights. They were traumatized as well. They stood with me, their mum. By Sunday, I got back to Abuja to get life started. I only collected my certificates and laptop. I left everything else. As a single lady, I had acquired some things for myself with which I had started a home with Eka. As time progressed, I acquired more things. I had no house, I had

117

In and Out

no idea of how and where to move my things. I left them. I hoped that there would be talks between Eka and I; talks on the way forward, especially regarding raising the children. Little did I know that Eka was least interested. I left my things hoping to be back for them. I was headed to Nyere's house. Nyere lived in a slum, but the slum had enormous peace.

On my way to Nyere's place, I pondered on why I had embarked on this fruitless journey. As soon as I thought it was fruitless, my inner voice chided me. "It wasn't fruitless, there are two beautiful seeds, remember?" I quickly retracted my thoughts. It was not fruitless, not at all, not with Kamsi and Nasa in the picture. Though children are gifts, those two were the most peaceful of children. They were the loveliest, the kindest and the greatest. I could not have traded them for anything. They did not deserve the harsh environment Eka and I were raising them in. Eka spoilt them with gifts. He tried to be a good dad. They never lacked anything. There was nothing their contemporaries had that they did not enjoy. Unfortunately, no respectable dad constantly abuses the mother of his children. A good dad is a good man. A good man is a good husband. This was my simple analogy.

"Why did I marry this man?" I asked myself again. "What was I expecting to get after seeing all the signs before marriage? Why did I not end it early? What kept me going for so long. Why did I linger to choose calmness over confusion? What were my fears? What was I protecting? What was I thinking? What was my gain?"

As I sat by myself at the back of the taxi on my way to Nyere's house. It was my long lonely path to freedom. The path I ought to have taken long before now. I looked back intermittently like someone who was unwilling to let go, tears ran down my cheeks. My shirt became

In and Out

drenched. "What could it have been that kept you Dinaka Chima?" I asked myself for the umpteenth time. Then the answer came; a song of Roxette. I hummed and sang and sobbed and wept …

The more I sang, the more I bowed my head. The more I cried, the more I regretted, and then the more I felt relieved. I raised my head, looked back again but we had driven a distance. The house was no longer in sight, not even the street. We were on the highway. There was a sharp rejig in my heart. I reflected. I wiped the tears and blew my nose. I adjusted my clothes and straightened my face with powder and lipstick. I repeated the last two lines of the song but no longer in tears…

What will I do next? Where will I start? Where would I live? How long would we be apart, the children and I? How will I fend for us? When will I measure up? How do I deal with the public? There was silence everywhere. No answers! I knew I was never really averse to divorce but I could not understand why it was not an easy choice for me. "At least you finally did, you finally found the courage, that's what matters" said the inner voice. I was happy as though I was doing something right for the first time in ten years. In the taxi, I looked bleak and hopeful at the same time. A new life thus began for me, a life of peace and tranquility. I lost my dad many years earlier. I often wondered how different things would have been if he were alive.

119

In and Out

I thought about my dad and the love I enjoyed from him. I remember him telling me that I was too simple for the jungle. He warned me that I should take care because I would not easily be understood. I regret he was gone. He was my first love. My dad, I was his replica. He loved me most out of his children. He did not hide it. We both knew it. For the first time in my life, I missed him greatly. He died two years before Eka came into my life. I missed him dearly. I promised him that I was going to be Dr Dinka Ezenna someday. I promised him that he would be at my graduation when I received my doctorate degree. He believed in me. Sickness did not allow our dreams materialize. He died. He left me to make life's decision. He left me to fall into Eka's hands. He left me. Maybe Eka would have respected him. My dad was vast and deep. He commanded respect. He was humorous. He was lovable. He was diplomatic. He was tall, huge and intimidating. He was handsome and learned. He was schooled in the defunct West Germany. He was exposed. He was liberal. He was calm. He was supportive and caring. He was rich. He was enlightened. he was wise. He was my hero.

Now I can tell that love is good but love is not enough. Love, the one that gives a butterfly-in-the-tummy feeling is insufficient to make a relationship work. Love is good but wisdom is better. I was unwise.

I spent quite a lot of my time in my imaginary world. Each spare moment was spent dreaming big and rebuilding my life. I saw myself happy. In my imagination, I mingled with the who is who. I was touching lives. I saw myself as a thought leader. I used my imprudence for other's benefit. "No one should tow this line", I constantly reminded myself. I finally embraced my new status as a single mum.

120

"My name is Dinaka Chima, formerly married with two beautiful children." I mastered introducing myself with that line.

In my new world, I was preparing for a wedding, a weeklong wedding, a heavenly wedding with the man of my dream - tall, dark, handsome, intelligent, caring, rich, generous, ambitious, fearless, liberal, supportive and wise. A man whose shoulder will be both for cuddling and climbing to my highest heights … the list was endless. It would be the mother of all weddings. Everything including the walls of the hotel we selected was bespoke. My dreams were without heights. Sometimes, I cried, other times, I laughed.

You may join me in my 'in-and-out' world.

In and Out

Glossary of *Igbo* phrases used

Asi m gi ba n'ulo	I said you should go back to the room
Dalu, dalu	thanks, thanks
Ebe ka I na-ga?	where are you headed?
Iboolachi	good morning
isi gini?	what did you say?
Nne m	my mother
Obim	my heart
Oga	boss
Ogo	in-law
Oso ahia	a process of making a quick sale without having stock

In and Out